# THE CANTOR'S VOICE

by

SOLOMON GISSER

Edited with an Introduction

by

David Patterson

Serviceberry Press
a division of
New South Architectural Press
Richmond, VA  Memphis, TN
2000

No part of this text may be reproduced without the permission of the author.
Copyright © 1997

ISBN 1-882595-15-7

In sacred memory of my parents and siblings so that we may never forget.

And for my children and grandchildren so that we may always remember.

# *Table of Contents*

Acknowledgements ............................................................. 6

Introductory Remarks ......................................................... 8

Growing Up Hungry ........................................................... 11

My Singing Career Begins ................................................. 17

My Adolescence ................................................................. 20

Strife in the Community as Shadows Loom ..................... 24

The Germans Invade Poland ............................................. 27

Forced into the Ghetto ....................................................... 30

Holy Days and Hunger ...................................................... 34

From the Ghetto to Camp to Camp .................................. 38

Auschwitz-Birkenau: *Arbeit Macht Frei* ......................... 50

A Strange Symphony ......................................................... 56

The Unfortunate Greeks .................................................... 59

Together with the Hungarian Jews .................................. 61

Unbelievable Tales of Escape ............................................ 69

Leaving Auschwitz: The Death March ............................ 73

Among the Dead in Buchenwald ..................................... 77

Ordruff ................................................................................. 82

Back to Buchenwald ........................................................... 86

| | |
|---|---|
| Workstat | 89 |
| Liberation | 92 |
| My Surviving Brothers | 99 |
| Chanting Prayers in Germany | 101 |
| Anna | 104 |
| Marriage and Family | 106 |
| At the Conservatory | 109 |
| Helen | 111 |
| Amsterdam | 115 |
| Going to Canada | 120 |
| David | 124 |
| My Other Brothers | 126 |
| Memories of My Mother and Father | 130 |
| Hyman and Sam | 134 |
| Aftermath | 138 |
| Final Reflections | 141 |
| About the Author | 142 |
| About the Editor | 143 |

# *Acknowledgements*

By profession, I am a singer, not a writer. The music and liturgy of the synagogue have always been a focal point in my life, reaching back to my childhood days in Poland as a choirboy soloist and, since the end of World War II, as a cantor in Germany, Holland, and for nearly fifty years in Montreal.

Throughout the painful tormented years of internment in Nazi concentration camps I never lost or forgot my passion for the music I loved; in many ways, I think it sustained me, perhaps playing its own part in giving me the will to continue and the hope that I might survive the ravages of the Holocaust.

For too many years, my family prodded me to document my experiences and to bear witness to what was and to what, I pray, will never be repeated. That prodding has resulted in this book. As in the case of many other survivors of the Holocaust, I humbly make this contribution to our collective memory of the darkest period in the history of the Jewish people.

While the experiences recorded in this book are mine, I wish to acknowledge, with many thanks, the invaluable assistance provided to me in bringing this book to fruition. I am indeed grateful to Dr. David Patterson, who holds the Bornblum Chair of Excellence in Judaic Studies at The University of Memphis and who has contributed his time and editorial skills to this book. I also wish to thank Ms. Sherry

Sucher and Dr. Joyce Rappaport, who also provided many hours of editorial input. Many thanks to my dear friends Dr. Jacob Rosensweig and Mindy Rosensweig (our friendship goes back to Dr. Rosensweig's days in Montreal) of Memphis, Tennessee, for their continued assistance, support, and encouragement in seeing this project through. My children deserve many thanks for their stubborn insistence and encouragement, as do my grandchildren, who have provided both the reason and the inspiraiton for this story to be told.

                                          Solomon Gisser

                                          December 1999

                                          Montreal, Canada

# *Introductory Remarks*

Both unique in its horror and universal in its implications, the Holocaust is the one event of the twentieth century that will perhaps decide our understanding of humanity for centuries to come. That is why humanity must make a decision in the light of the questions and the testimony it confronts within the depths of this event. What lies in those depths? A silent outcry. How are we to hear it? Through the voices of survivors like Solomon Gisser—through the cantor's voice. Precisely this is most striking about Solomon Gisser's memoir: it comes to us as a cantor's voice and therefore as the voice not only of memory but of prayer—as a voice of the holy and of the Holy One who addresses us in prayer even as we address Him. *That* is what was targeted for annihilation in the Holocaust; that is what makes the Holocaust the Holocaust.

The Nazis who prohibited Jewish existence also prohibited Jewish prayers. Indeed, one is interwoven with the other:

without their prayers—without their teaching and tradition, their memory and meaning—Jews have no existence. Setting out to silence Jewish prayer, the Nazis set out to silence God Himself. For God speaks through Jewish prayer. When Jews cry out the prayer, "*Shema Yisrael*—Hear, O Israel," God pleads with humanity to hear. Why did the Nazis set out to murder not only the body of Israel but its teaching and tradition, its memory and meaning—its very soul? Because if the Führer's word is to be law and reality (as the great German philosopher Martin Heidegger declared), then God's word must be silenced. And one way to silence God's word is to erase from the world Jewish presence and Jewish prayers.

But the Jewish prayers through which God's word reverberates within the world were not silenced. Solomon Gisser's memoir attests to that. Written by a man who has every rational reason to fall silent in the face of a world that was silent, this memoir not only breaks a silence—it summons a voice, from above and below. Both eloquent and insightful, Gisser's style is at once conversational and cantorial; he does not just tell his story—he conveys his urgency and thus offers his testimony. To be sure, in *The Cantor's Voice* Gisser does more than speak—he *chants*, his words rising up to the heavens on a column of smoke and ash that continues to cast its shadow over the face of the earth. Hearing his impassioned chant, his readers become a congregation as they come into the presence of this memory. Like prayers, the words that form this memory are at once simple and profound. Like prayers, Gisser's words lead us through a realm in which prayers too struggle for their existence, if only to to engage God in a struggle, as Jacob did at Peniel.

Gisser's struggle and his preparation for the struggle began from the time of his birth in 1918. His earliest memoirs of a childhood in Poland are memories of hunger. Yet they are memories filled with love, memories of the sanctity of life that he struggled to take with him through the concentrationary universe, from ghetto to camp after camp. Many of the names that shape this memory will be familiar, names like Lodz, Auschwitz, and Buchenwald. But other names—the names of camps like Belitz, Neustadt, Kreutze, Dretz, Babitz, and Ordruff—may not be so familiar. Like the details about "life" in the Lodz Ghetto, the details related to those camps make Gisser's memoir an important contribution not only to testimony but also to history. His many tales of the human beings who lived and died in those places, moreover, put a face to that history. They are tales of miracles and wonders, of good and evil, of people struggling to live through their own death. In a word, they are tales of a humanity that would not die.

Gisser's continuing struggle to sustain a remnant of humanity underscores yet another important dimension of his memoir of the Holocaust: the memoir shows how the death manufactured in the anti-world of Auschwitz spills over into the post-war world. Through stories such as the tale of his wedding that had everything except family, Gisser explores the survivor's difficulty in leaving the camps behind even after he has left them. His memoir thus calls into question any triumphant talk of liberation, if liberation means returning to a home and a family and dwelling place in the world. That is precisely where the reader of the memoir comes in. For dwelling happens where one person listens as another person speaks. It happens where those who hear a testimony are transformed into witnesses. It happens where we strive to add our voices to the cantor's voice.

David Patterson
Bornblum Chair in Judaic Studies
The University of Memphis
January 2000

# Growing Up Hungry

I was born in Warsaw in 1918 into a life of sheer misery. I have no memory of ever having enough food or clothing. Had it not been for my aunt, who came to take me to her home each day to feed me, I might not have survived. I was also told she couldn't feed me fast enough because I always cried between mouthfuls.

I grew up in a house with a very religious atmosphere. We were ten children, and I was the seventh. My father's name was Moses—Moshe in Hebrew. He was born in Radom, Poland, in 1883 to a Hasidic family and had spent his youth studying in *yeshivot* (Jewish religious schools). In those days, people studied not to become rabbis but to learn Torah just for the sake of discovering and knowing its richness. The opportunity to become a rabbi wasn't even a consideration for my father. I remember him always as a scholar. He was not a business man, but was constantly studying, poring over the Talmud. He was shy and quiet, but when he talked, people listened with great interest. For he was a scholarly man. He never shouted, and he had a very good nature. This world didn't mean very much to him.

Even though my father knew the Talmud inside and out, he had to go to work. Through his business, he traveled as a young man to Warsaw; and it was there that he met my mother, who lived with her family. As soon as my father saw her, he admired her, and it wasn't a long time before he received her dowry from my grandfather. My mother, whose name was Sarah Golda, married my father when she was seventeen years old, in Warsaw. She was the daughter of a very religious Hasidic man. His name was Rothenberg, and he was well-known in Warsaw, a city that had 400,000 Jews.

My mother had three brothers and one sister. Her father made a livelihood by making cartons. Like my father, my mother was studious. She came from a house of learning, and could speak and write Hebrew well. My relatives recalled that when my father was taken to the army to fight in the Japanese War, she wrote a letter in Hebrew to the Rabbi of Moscow to free my father from the army. The rabbi apparently showed her letter to his friends, because he was so impressed at receiving such intelligent words from so young a woman (she must have been no more than eighteen). She was also a very sensitive woman, and she was very beautiful too.

My father ran a business in Warsaw for a short time. Unfortunately, he wasn't a great businessman and the times were rough. He couldn't maintain a family in Warsaw, so he ended up moving to Lodz, where his sister Esther lived. I was a year old. Esther was married to a wealthy man who sold dry goods and materials. She was the aunt who saved me from starvation by feeding me, they tell me, large portions of cream of wheat (to this very day I still like it). My father tried to work for his brother-in-law, but this business association didn't last for long either.

He tried many times to establish himself in the business world, but he never succeeded. He simply was not a good businessman. Even though he made a living, he earned the very, very minimum, and it was hard for him to support our large family. It wasn't until my oldest sister developed her skills and got a position as a bookkeeper that we were a little better off. Indeed, she and my brother ended up supporting the whole family.

My oldest sister was Rosa. After her came Isaac, Eva, Mordechai, David, Meyer, myself, Hyman (who, like me, is a cantor in Montreal), and Sam. Feivel, my youngest brother, came to Auschwitz and unfortunately was taken to the crematorium. Nearly all of my brothers and sisters were killed by the Nazis.

My family, teachers, and friends discovered my talent as a singer when I was very young. People knew from their friends that I could sing. When I was a little boy, I simply liked to sing. I must have been just four years old when I went to a little school, a *cheder*, and I remember that the teacher put me up on the table and said, "Sing. We heard that you know how to sing." At home we sang every day for guests. We were a musical family, and little by little we got to be known as singers. Eventually this led to my brother and me being invited to sing in a choir.

But singing was a luxury. My family was very poor. We could not think about fineries like music lessons, and we experienced the worst kind of depression that one can imagine. In 1929 there was a depression in the United States, but my family had never known anything but depression in the worst way. We considered anybody who had enough to eat to be a rich person. And we were not a family that had enough to eat.

Nonetheless, I somehow grew up even with all these difficulties. When I say with difficulties, I mean that when I went to school every other child had lunch, but I didn't. I was hungry. When you are hungry you can't study very well. So I wasn't one of the better students.

The children in my family did not receive much education. In fact, my brothers started to work right after elementary school. My sisters went to school, but since we lived in a house without electricity, they didn't have enough light to do their homework. I remember how they used to go downstairs because a gas lantern in the street shone in our window and enabled them to study. They didn't have their own books, but had to borrow from friends late at night. Books were too expensive for my family to afford.

My oldest sister was a brilliant student despite these hardships. But she had to leave school to go to work when she was about fifteen or sixteen. She learned bookkeeping and went to work for a distant cousin who ran a silk business. Eventually, she became a bookkeeper for the entire Lodz ghetto.

Our small house in Lodz, where we lived before the war, had one big room and a kitchen. For ten children and two parents, it was very crowded. But somehow we managed. And the housing conditions weren't our biggest misfortunes. Our main misery was that there was never enough money to buy food.

The age span between my oldest sister and me was twelve years. There were always little ones in the house. My mother stayed home and took care of us, doing the cooking and housework.

We were very close. My parents were kind of aristocratic in their dignity. Even though they were Hasidic, they were modern and worldly. They were not ultra orthodox fanatics. We didn't have *payes*, the earlocks that very religious Jewish boys and men never trim. We were brought up to keep in touch with Western secular values as well.

But the economic strains of the times took their toll on my family. I was a worrier from the earliest times, always dreading events that possibly could befall my family. I worried endlessly about my two older sisters, whose chances for marriage were so very limited because we were poor. In those days, if a girl didn't have a dowry, she could rarely expect to get married. Times were very bad, and if a poor boy wanted to marry, his station in life and his ability to rise economically depended upon his wife's dowry. No matter how beautiful the girl was, this was the economic reality, the way it was.

I remember hushed voices and endless conversations about this situation. It became an obsession for me. And people noticed how troubled I had become. Because of my endless worrying, I acquired the nickname, the *nadn ponim*, or "dowry face!" My sad face always reflected my worry about my sisters. The lack of money for their dowries dominated many discussions in our home.

But when I was about twelve, my sister somehow had saved up enough money to marry. She went out with a boy, and they got married. I remember feeling a heavy weight being lifted off our family. But then I began to worry about my younger sister, Eva. There seemed to be no chance that she could ever afford to marry.

One day, however, something incredible happened that affected our circumstances in a positive way. My mother's brother, Chaim Yudel, was a kind of show off who manufactured paper boxes for a living. It wasn't an easy business, though for awhile he did quite well. However, he began to lose money because he constantly borrowed from others. Eventually, he went bankrupt and had to go back to Warsaw. He then developed tuberculosis, and was sent by the government to a sanitorium.

After he recovered, he never gave up hope about becoming wealthy again. He never failed to buy a lottery ticket. He would have sold everything he owned to buy lottery tickets! Usually he lost his money, but one Saturday he came to the *shtiebl,* the small synagogue he used to attend, and as usual greeted a man who had sold him a quarter part of a lottery ticket. My uncle asked if the "million" zlotis prize ticket had been drawn yet.

The man replied, "Yes, yes, but you didn't win."

But my uncle persisted in asking again. The man replied impatiently, "I told you, you didn't win."

But my uncle insisted on knowing the number of the winning ticket. This conversation took place in the middle of the service, while the Torah was being read aloud in a supposedly pious atmosphere. And when my uncle heard what the number was, he crashed onto the floor, passing out with excitement. It was *his* number that had won a million zlotis, and he was entitled to a quarter of the prize. In those days a zloti was worth more than a dollar.

After this, my family's economic situation changed. Our kind uncle was suddenly a millionaire! How impressed we were. And because he was a very good-natured man, he helped us out. He gave his two brothers and two sisters 5000 zlotis each.

When my parents received their 5000 zlotis in cash, they put aside 3000 for Eva's dowry. With the other 2000, they were able to pay their bills and rent for awhile. But in the end, even this amount wasn't enough money to live on. My father wasn't working, and the only ones who were able to earn a living were my sister and my older brother. And they still weren't earning enough to pay the rent once the lottery money was gone.

Knowing that we had 3000 zlotis put away, my parents borrowed from my sister's money. They borrowed so much that soon there was nothing left. She never got married, which was a tragedy for a Jewish girl in those days.

# *My Singing Career Begins*

My brother Meyer and I were quite talented, and we sang all the time. When I was eight and he was ten, we decided that we wanted to join a choir. Since Lodz was a city with 275,000 Jews, there were potentially many synagogues for us to go to.

Somebody told us that we should talk to the choir leader at one of the largest synagogues, the old City Synagogue (in Yiddish, the *Alt-Statische Shul*). One day my sister Rosa took us both to try to locate this choir leader. At the synagogue, we were greeted by a man with a beard; he was the sexton, or *shammes*, of the synagogue. We asked where we could find the choir leader. The shammes very politely directed us to an address nearby, and we went there immediately, hoping to thrill the man with our voices.

The choir leader's apartment was on the fourth floor of a depressing residence. He lived in a damp, dark room in the attic. It was the type of place where people usually would hang their laundry to dry. The ceiling was very low, even for two children who weren't so tall. We had to bow our heads in order to get inside and across to him.

By the time we opened the door, it had grown almost dark both outside and inside. We looked around the room but it was hard to see anything. Finally, we saw the outline of a very short, thin man sitting near the window. The whole apartment was very shabby and very dark, and he was sitting at the window, writing music upon a small table. Near him on the right side was a spittoon and on the table was a pile of white music paper. He sat there smoking; an empty bottle of vodka was on the table next to him.

He wrote, wrote, and wrote, seemingly oblivious to any intrusion. When we came up to him, he finally looked up and inquired, not unpleasantly, "What would you like? Why are you here?"

My sister told him that we were two brothers who happened to be very talented at singing. "Would it be possible for my brothers to join your choir?" He responded by saying, "Very good. It's a possibility if they have good voices. Let them come to see me the next time I have a rehearsal in the synagogue."

He told us a date and time, and promised to give us an audition. If he liked us, we would be allowed to join the choir. And naturally, he said, we would get paid too. When we heard these words, it was for us as if the Messiah had already come. So we went home cheerful and full of anticipation.

At the designated time, my other sister Eva took us over to the synagogue. The choir leader asked us to sing a selection, and we did so, first myself and then my brother. The choir master liked us so much that he said, "You are going to be my soloists."

We had very beautiful alto voices, and in addition to this, our two voices blended so well whenever we sang together that people thought we were one voice. We were very happy with our new singing careers, although the poverty continued to be in our way all the time.

There was a man named Zilberschatz who lived in Lodz. I remember his name after so many years because he did something unique for us. He was a bachelor, and he always listened to my brother and me when we sang together. One day he stood waiting for us outside the synagogue, and he approached us, saying, "Are you the two who sang solo together today?" We said yes, to which he replied, "Tomorrow, I want you to come to a certain restaurant."

The place he named was really a cafe where people came to sip beer and eat salty pretzels while listening to records featuring great cantors. It was a special place called Nussn Farber's Restaurant.

We arrived there the next day, hungry as usual, and were overwhelmed when Zilberschatz told us to *eat all we wanted*, and that he would pay for us! This was an unimaginable treat for us, because we had always craved the goodies in the store window. How could we ever have had enough money to buy such treats?

We didn't know whether to regard Zilberschatz as an angel or a human. And he returned to the restaurant with us practically every Sunday. At the same time, we got to listen to cantorial records.

# My Adolescence

I celebrated my bar mitzvah at the end of the summer, in 1931. At that time, we were living out in the country; it wasn't far from Lodz but it was definitely not an urban area. It would have been called a suburb today. My father prayed, or *davened*, each morning in a little house where a *rebbe* sold the *aliyahs*; that is, the people paid the rabbi for the privilege of being called up to the Torah to recite a prayer. The *minyan* (ten men, the minimum number for public prayer services) was in his house, so through selling aliyahs he could sustain himself and pay the rent.

I turned thirteen and was supposed to get a *maftir aliyah*, the last call-up to the Torah. I expected to recite the Haftorah, too, which is a passage usually from the Prophets, that follows the Torah reading. But these honours apparently were reserved for richer people than my father. As an adult today, of course, I don't blame them, for this rebbe had to make a living.

Instead of receiving the final special honour aliyah, I received a regular aliyah. I am a Levi, so they gave me the second aliyah, and I was deprived of getting the maftir. And God knows what a gorgeous voice I already had; my voice had changed and I could have chanted so beautifully. I was already reading the Torah at that point. It was a big disappointment for me, but what could I have done? Later that Saturday afternoon, ten boys came over for candy and cake. This was my modest bar mitzvah. I couldn't have wished for more.

Shortly after my bar mitzvah, the economic situation in Lodz grew even worse. There was a terrific depression, so my parents and my older siblings determined that I had to earn money to contribute what little I could to the family finances. So I had to quit school and went into a little business of my own.

My business consisted of buying little pieces of waste scraps from the tailors. The tailors themselves were very poor, but even they didn't charge me for those little threadworn pieces, because they had already thrown them away into the garbage.

I must have looked like quite a sight. Sometimes I would even crawl into in their attics to lie on the floor, breathing dust and gathering up little pieces of cloth that had probably been lying there for years. I breathed in the filthy dust all day long, and finally would gather together a sack that would weigh about fifteen or twenty kilos. Then I would bring the scraps to a wholesaler.

On luckier days, I would gather up material of a higher quality, and I would get a little more money for it. But on other days, the quality was worse and I hardly earned a cent.

And when I was paid approximately two zlotis at the end of the day, I would run home quickly. As soon as I entered the doorway, I would give the money to my mother. How happy this made me feel. It meant that for the next day, we wouldn't have to worry; there was sure to be a nice breakfast for us.

My singing sustained me spiritually over these hard times.

I didn't regard myself as a merchant selling used scraps of cloth; no, during this time I still had the love of my life, my singing. Yet even singing had its hardships and embarrassments. With pride, I agreed to perform concerts, but many times when there was a concert and I was asked to sing, I didn't have a decent suit to wear. I borrowed suits from others, but since my arms were unusually long, the sleeves of the suit were always too short. I would be singing and feeling so uncomfortable, not knowing how to cover my arms.

When I was about sixteen, I could read music and belonged to an organization, a club called HaZamir. *Zamir* means "to sing." My voice had of course already changed, and I was now a baritone. I had many opportunities to sing with them.

This organization performed works by Haydn, Verdi, Berlioz, Handel, and so on, with everything in Hebrew. Later on, in 1938, we performed the whole *La Traviata* in Yiddish. I hope there are others alive who remember this event. Our conductor, whose name was Izaac Sacks, was a genius. He conducted the whole opera by heart even though he hadn't even been an opera conductor before. But he was a great genius who composed works that were out of this world. I remember sitting in his home, in a hotel called the Hotel Polonia. I wrote out every part from his *La Traviata* score. As I copied it out, I sang it, and for this reason I can still conduct the whole opera today by heart. When you are young, you remember things better.

I sang with HaZamir for a long time; my voice became stronger and nicer. I had learned to sightread at twelve; I was exceptional in this field, for even the tenors and the basses often didn't know how to read music. This proved to be a great advantage for me.

There were two rehearsals a week. One day, Professor Sacks asked if I could lead the rehearsal once a week, for the women's section. I undertook this project gladly, and worked diligently, very hard, to rehearse with and coach them. This experience proved to be invaluable later on.

I also coached a private student in sightreading. Her name was Sturma and she had moved to Lodz from Bialystock, with her parents. She happened to be gorgeous. She was beautiful beyond any description. And somehow she liked me very much. I would often take her home, trying to arrive at her residence before eleven p.m. before the gates were closed (we would have had to pay 10 cents for the janitor to open them after this time).

One day, she invited me to give her a lesson at her house. To my surprise, her parents were out of town and we were alone. Immediately, my heart began to pound. I had never felt anything like this before, and I didn't know what to do with myself. I was terribly, terribly shy. Coming from a home like mine, it was unthinkable for me to fall in love with her. But I *was* in love. To show it, however, was a different story.

She said, "Why don't you sit down? Try to make yourself comfortable."

I sat down. But my heart didn't stop pounding, and she saw how uncomfortable I was.

Then she said, "Don't think about lessons today. Let's talk and enjoy ourselves."

To my luck, she took out a cigarette and said, "Do you have a match?"

I said, "No, but there's a store not far from here and I will go out and buy one."

I went out to buy a match. But I never returned. And to this very day, with everything that has happened since, both tragic and trivial, I will never forgive myself for what I had done. She was so angry after this incident that I could hardly make peace with her again. And unfortunately this gorgeous, gorgeous girl went back to Bialystock before the Germans came, before the ghetto, and I heard later that the Nazis had killed her.

# Strife in the Community as Shadows Loom

How tragic it is, in retrospect, to note how divided the Jewish community of Lodz could sometimes be. We were being pounded by the rise of Nazism, and yet we ourselves could not stop arguing about religious issues.

I remember a story about an old synagogue that was probably built in 1850. The old cantor of this synagogue passed away, and the synagogue sought to hire another cantor. They auditioned various singers, but the search was not easy. Cantors had to be both qualified and personable. The synagogue's congregation looked for personality and for piety.

One Friday night we arrived at the synagogue, and found that the choir leader, our trainer, was completely drunk. He was always drunk, it was true, but not to the extent of that evening. A tenor from the choir had to take over instead, and the regular leader sat down.

All of a sudden, we were glimpsing up at a tall, handsome new cantor. He was about to begin the service when we heard a terrible, terrible noise. Apparently, two sides of people had begun fighting. There were people who wanted very much to hear the new cantor, and there were people who were furious and were against hiring him in principle (I will soon explain why they were opposed to him).

There was a lot of commotion, a lot of yelling in the room. Suddenly the shammes, the man who was supposed to maintain order and dignity in the synagogue, raised a gavel and fiercely banged on the table until the people finally stopped their nearly vicious squabbling.

They were still not completely silent, but then the visiting cantor suddenly totally silenced them when he uttered the first phrase from the Friday night service. His voice was so beautiful, so gorgeous that the people—even those who didn't want him to be present—listened with awe. We started singing along with him. At the end of the service, he made *kiddush*, taking a cup of wine and singing the necessary blessings, and we accompanied him. At one point he sang a high D over the high C: his voice contained a brilliance that no one could have imagined.

Everybody wondered who he was. We finally found out that his name was Simcha Koussevitsky, younger brother of the great cantor Moshe Koussevitsky (no relation to Sergei Koussevitsky of Vilna). He was one of four brothers, each one unusually talented.

The next day, we learned with shame what the fight had been about. When we arrived in the morning to sing, the doors to the synagogue were locked. I looked on and felt disgust when I saw that everyone was standing outside, fighting and screaming. This was a synagogue! It was a place where everyone was supposedly welcome to worship.

It wasn't a place for the VIPS from the city, but it was popular with the tailors and shoemakers and peddlers—the workers.

Why had they closed the synagogue? Because the leadership of the city were quite orthodox, and they didn't like the idea of a cantor who didn't have a beard. Every cantor in the past had had a beard and had been very religious.

It didn't matter that this new cantor, too, was very religious. Since he didn't have a beard he wouldn't be allowed to serve in this synagogue. To avoid having to see him, the opposition group locked the doors and didn't let the people in. Furthermore, we heard that the people went to the houses of the leaders, breaking windows and doing rampant damage.

This was the only time that this synagogue was closed for a Saturday morning service. Many people today don't know that episodes like this took place before the war. And how awful, how petty it seems in retrospect. How were we all to know what the Nazis would soon do to each Jew who was there that night, bearded or beardless.

Too soon, I began to feel the Nazi fate looming over synagogue life in Lodz.

# *The Germans Invade Poland*

When the German troops overran Poland in 1939, life as we knew it came to a sudden stop. My family huddled together, wondering what to do. Should we try to escape? With fear, we debated the pros and cons of every possible act.

Fate has strange ways, strange trivial ways of determining our everyday acts. I don't know now if it was for the good or the bad, but the night the Germans came in with their pounding artillery, I was sick with dysentery. Some of the people in our neighbourhood ran out and tried to escape, but my family decided to remain in our rooms because I couldn't get up from bed.

We never wanted to be separated. My mother always wanted to have her children there with her. As a parent now, I understand her wishes, but ultimately our decisions to remain together were perhaps not right. If a few of us had been able to escape alone before the war, a few more of us might have survived.

But this was our destiny, and because of me none of us ran out. Some of the people who did run away were shot anyway; they couldn't get away from the German Messerschmidt airplanes that were loaded with artillery.

The tragedy had been building up for years, but it truly began in full force when the Germans invaded Poland and established the ghettos. We lived at that time in a house that was not too comfortable, but our standard of living was considered decent. At that time, we had electricity.

When I was twenty-one years old, I sang at a major synagogue called the Deutsche Synagogue. Here we would call its style Reform, but at that time there was no Reform temple in Lodz. The Jews who went to the Deutsche Synagogue were rich and removed from the Orthodox class. But I sang in that *shul* and I can vividly remember one morning when my brother and I made our way across town. This was in late autumn of 1939, when the ghetto was not yet established and we were working for Germans who had taken over the Jewish businesses.

As we approached the synagogue, we witnessed our first major act of Nazi destruction. In horror, we watched as the synagogue was burned to the ground.

The Germans were gathered about the building that morning, and suddenly we realized that the shul was burning. Red flames leapt madly from the inside. It was still a little dark outside, and we watched, both wearing the Star of David on the front and back of our clothing. How sad and desperate we felt, afraid to look left or right. We saw the greatest synagogue, the most beautiful one in Lodz, and one of the most beautiful of synagogues everywhere, as it burned to the ground. This wasn't the synagogue where I usually sang, but it was a major synagogue of the Jewish community.

The one in which I usually sang was located in what was to become the Ghetto, and it too was eventually dynamited in the summer of 1940.

# Forced into the Ghetto

The call to leave for the Ghetto came in the beginning of 1940, in January or February. There were announcements posted all over town, saying that we had to leave our houses to go to a certain slum area in Lodz. Almost everybody had somebody—a poor relative, an impoverished friend—living there, so we had an idea of what our current fate was going to be.

Moving, being forced to move, was the biggest tragedy I could have imagined up to that point. We were allowed to bring only the barest necessities with us; everything else had to be left at home. And so we gave up our home, and went to live in an environment suited only for animals.

People came into the ghetto using any means they could; we piled our few possessions into little wagons. It was a scene out of hell that I don't even want to describe.

When we came into the ghetto, we had to find a place to

live. It was not hard to find a family who took us in, even though we were three families in one room, a big room with no plumbing. The plumbing and toilets were downstairs in the courtyard. It was gruesome to live like this in the cold Polish winters. The winters were harsh, very harsh. It was a time of catastrophe.

In the beginning, the ghetto wasn't yet closed. My brother and I continued to work for two Germans whom we had known before, so we were still able to earn a little bit of a living.

The Germans for whom we worked had changed, however. Since their occupation of Lodz, they had grown into bigshots. With glee, they took over the businesses of those for whom they used to work. We worked for a company that owned knitting machines. My brother was a cutter and I was a clerk.

But the work and its meagre salaries did not allow us to eat. The tragedy of starvation started soon enough. The food in the ghetto was limited and hard to purchase, even if one had money. The potatoes were rotten and frozen.

People were dying, first by the hundreds, and later by the thousands, every single day. It was inhuman in the Lodzer ghetto, as well as in the other ghettoes.

One day we had absolutely nothing to eat. We sat starving, all of us in the room, and even though there was a little iron stove with pipes for transmitting heat, we needed fuel or coal, and we didn't have any wood. Out of desperation, my brother Meyer and I went to a construction site. I took a saw and we started cutting up the wood. We cut enough wood for a month.

It was the middle of the night, and we thought nobody would hear or see us. The building site was not far from our house. We went in and started sawing a large beam, first on one side and then on the other side.

But we were wrong in thinking that no one had heard us. The police heard us. And they were even crueller than we imagined, for they waited until we had just about finished our job. They were the ghetto police, the Jewish police. They were afraid of their superiors and they acted worse than the real police. And God forbid, if they caught somebody, they took him or her to the Criminal Polizei, to the real authorities. Then they would throw the offender into a special jail.

People never came out alive from the jail; they were tortured to death. The prisoners who were sent there wrote about their torture upon the prison walls.

The police came in and caught us. Ironically, they made us finish our cutting and sawing, because they wanted us to take the beam for themselves. It was quite heavy, and they made both of us carry it to the police station.

Luckily for us, there was a young man at the station, who had heard and seen me conduct a choir in the soup kitchen. He himself was somewhat musically inclined, so he begged the other police to spare our lives and not send us to prison.

He said, "Please let them go home. It is enough that they brought us the wood." We went home to sleep. We should have been feeling fortunate that we were still alive. But our hearts were crying; we were cold, so cold. We were only relieved because we hadn't been sent to the ghetto jail.

We were desperate. One day my delicate father, of blessed memory, was very sick with gallstones. It was terrible to hear him screaming in pain. There were no doctors around, and if there were indeed any in town, we couldn't reach them. The house was so cold that you could see the snow on the walls. And he was lying in bed, hungry like the rest of us. There was nothing in the house to eat. And if there was something to buy, we didn't have the money to buy it. We spent the whole day sitting and swallowing saliva. It was the worst day I had ever experienced until that point.

What did I do? I reminded myself that I knew a girl who worked for Chaim Rumkowski, the German-appointed "leader" whom we all called "King of the Ghetto." Rumkowski was the most hated leader we could have had, but his connections to the Germans gave him all sorts of privileges. I knew that the woman I had in mind was better off than we were, so I decided to ask her for some bread.

It took a lot of courage, but it was already dark so I decided to forget about my pride. I went over to where she lived, and she was very glad to see me. I said with a tone that wasn't my usual calm voice, "Listen, I didn't come here to socialize. I just want to ask you one question: can you lend me a bread or a half a bread. We don't have anything at home."

Right away she went over to her cupboard and cut off a quarter for herself and three quarters for me, saying, "Go, take it home."

I didn't even say more than "thank you" to her because all I wanted to do was to run home. To this day, I don't know how I ran home so quickly. When I came into the house, I saved the whole family from starvation. And everyone in the family got a piece; it was like distributing a million, no, a billion dollars to a poor person.

But that was not the way I wanted to live. I was furious. I was humiliated. Things had to change.

That night, my brother and I decided to register to go to Germany for volunteer work. Little did we know about what really was happening to the Jews who had left the ghetto. It wasn't until we arrived in a camp that we realized where we were. But that's a story for later.

# Holy Days and Hunger

Even in the ghetto, there were times that I recall as warm or pleasant. In 1940, the VIPS of the community were honoured with a special service that took place in the soup kitchen. There were many soup kitchens in our community, but a special one was established for the "aristocratic" Jews: professionals, lawyers, doctors, and leaders who were associated with the so-called government.

The VIPS decided to hold high holiday services that fall, and they asked a cantor with one of the most beautiful voices to lead the service. Fortunately this cantor, Abraham Brun, survived the war and is still alive; he now lives in Long Beach, New York. I was hired to organize a choir to accompany him, and I was able to put together a group of excellent singers. Because all of the synagogues of Lodz had already been mercilessly destroyed, I was able to choose the best singers from each congregation.

Our performance was supreme. We even had the distinct pleasure of having Chaim Rumkowski come to our service. For us, this was an honour. Few choirs sound so good today. The whole ghetto talked about our service for weeks on end.

Even today, some people have heard of this performance. By coincidence, a professor of political science who lived in Montreal called me to say that he had found a book about the Lodz ghetto. In it was my advertisement announcing the high holiday service. In three languages—Polish, Yiddish, and German, it announces the appearance of Cantor Avraham Brun, conducted by Solomon Gisser.

After the holidays, we expected to be paid, as we had been promised. The singers hadn't expected to sing for nothing; they were all hungry. And since I was the choir leader, it was my duty to collect our salaries from a man by the name of Prashker.

But when I went to his office and tried to enter the premises, I was prevented by a policeman at the door. Prashka claimed to be busy. What he did there, God knows, but he was busy. And I stood outside there for one hour, and then for two hours. I was hungry and cold in the autumn air. Finally, the door opened and I thought Prashka was ready to see me.

I started to enter the office, but he would not let me in. He looked at me with a condescending air, and snorted, "I'm sorry, but I have no time today." I was furious, and yelled back, "What do you mean, you have no time?" But before I even finished speaking, the door was slammed shut again, and I stood like a dog behind it, waiting for it to open up. But nothing happened.

My rage increased and I did something totally out of character for me. That is what hunger and humiliation can do to a person. I smashed my foot against the door, kicking it with such force that it banged opened. Even Prashka looked scared.

I demanded with force, "What do you mean? Do you know

that my singers have to get paid? That they are all starving? You know we did a magnificent job and you promised to pay us. I want to get paid *now*." There was silence in the tense room.

Finally, I got a reaction, though it was not what I had expected. Instead of cash, they decided to give us soup for a whole month in the kitchen. Maybe they did not know it, but this part of the payment was the best reward we could have received. Each time we had free soup, it was a God-send.

But this was one of the rare events that turned out well. More often, in the times that followed, we stood in the regular soup kitchen and waited a whole night to be able to be closer to the door when it opened in the morning. There were so many times that I stood with my brothers and sisters, waiting in the cold, the snow, or the rain for hours. Sometimes the stronger ones pushed themselves in, grabbing all the food, leaving us with nothing when we finally reached the head of the distribution lines.

And we were not the only ones standing and waiting. Some people passed out from starvation, and some died.

The ghetto was a scene of unbelievable starvation. People may think that ghetto residents were better off and had more freedom than the Jews in the concentration camps. But in terms of nutrition, the ghetto was even worse than Auschwitz. At least when we came to a camp we knew that we would be given soup once a day, sometimes twice.

But there were no guarantees in the ghetto. The quality of the food that the Germans sent in was the worst. To tempt us, in addition, there were young little boys, maybe eight or nine years old, who sold candies in the street illegally. We didn't know where they got them, but they advertised these candies by calling out to us with their sweet singing voices. The children would charge five cents for each bag. But when a policeman saw the children selling these sweets, the children would run away, dropping the candies, and he would chase the children. Then the policeman would throw all the candies into the sewer while we stood by, starving.

Ironically, people would say that in the ghetto, horsemeat had become *kosher* and candy had become *traif*. Horsemeat, forbidden to Jews by religious law, was something the Nazis allowed us to eat, even while they tossed our kosher candies into the sewers.

One needed a license to sell candy, but horsemeat was just fine. The irony was that those miserable beasts (the Germans, for they acted like beasts and were no different than animals) went out of their way to send in horsemeat for Jews who were forbidden to touch it. They made us eat horsemeat, those of us who could scrape together enough money to buy it. This was kosher but candies were not.

My family did not have enough money to buy even the horsemeat. And even if we had had the money, we wouldn't have bought it. My father was a very religious man, and he would not allow nonkosher meat in our house, even during the worst of times. This was his policy even when horsemeat was officially allowed by the rabbinate. When life is at stake, even nonkosher food is permitted, because life is precious. Life comes first. Nevertheless, we never touched it. We ate nothing instead.

# *From the Ghetto to Camp to Camp*

The Germans who governed the ghetto had promised that the families of volunteers to Germany would receive 90 marks a month. If my brother and I volunteered, our family would receive 180 marks. This would surely help them. For us to sit at home, without employment and without food, seemed increasingly useless to us.

And we couldn't stand it anymore. That night when I had to beg for bread it really broke my resistance; there were other terrible things too—too terrible to talk about. So we decided that we would volunteer to go away.

Going away was not easy. But when the day came, we refused to change our minds, even though our mother's heart was breaking.

We were taken to an *Umschlagplatz,* a neutral place that was still in ghetto territory. Saying goodbye to my parents, my brothers, and my sisters was the most terrible event in my life. My father was so sick in bed that he couldn't even come out. And my mother, with whom we were so close, knew that she would never see us again. My mother never wanted anyone to go away. I remember before the war, that my brother wanted to go to France because the situation in Poland was very bad, and she refused to let him go. She would never let any of her sons or daughters go away from us. And this was ultimately a very big mistake.

We could only imagine what was in their hearts, and they in ours. We traveled for many hours. We were taken away to a place called RAB Lager (*Reichsautobahn Lager*), located in Neutomischel. We were told that we were supposed to work on the freeway, the beginning of the German Autobahn, in Oberschlesien.

It didn't look too bad at first. The barracks were new; indeed, everything there was new because we were the first arrivals. We organized ourselves a bit, and they gave us something to eat.

But then they asked us to form a column. The German who was the head of the camp gave us a speech, and by the time he was finished, we knew that we were prisoners, not just volunteers. He finished this speech by screaming out with venom: "You are going to sweat here with blood. If you think you have come to a sanitorium or to a picnic, you have made a big mistake."

We were in a forest, and when the German officer finished speaking, he took a piece of wood, marched up ferociously to a man who was in his way, took the block of wood, and knocked the man over the head. The man fell down. I don't know if he lived very long afterwards.

We were all young people. Some were a little older, some a little younger, some in their late twenties, some in their early twenties. We were all men, and the Germans needed workers. The incident in the forest was the first encounter we had with our true fate. With this incident, we really knew where we were. And then one hardship after another followed, one tragedy after the other.

Eventually we were moved to Camp Belitz, not far from Frankfurt on the Oder (not Frankfurt-am-Main). There were no comforts there. I tried only to console myself with prayer. I was there when it was Purim (the holiday in late winter observed in remembrance of the deliverance of the Jews as told in the Book of Esther), and we wanted to read the Megilla, the Book of Esther, that is read aloud on this festival. How fitting it was to read of the Jewish people's horrific experiences in Persia, and then of their redemption.

There were two hundred Jews in the camp, and we tried to figure out how to recite the Megilla without a text. There were some very knowledgeable boys among us, but reading the Megilla takes special skill. Since I had a photographic memory, and knew how to read the Torah, I also had learned to read the Megilla at a very young age. I had chanted it before I was thirteen: at the age of twelve, I had read it to an elderly woman who was unable to get to the synagogue. I had gone to her house where she had given me a piece of cake (I just waited for the next year to do the same!). So, in the camp, I volunteered to chant the Megilla by heart for those two hundred people. I recited the ten chapters, and still remember them perfectly today.

The Megilla reading was one of the rare happy events at that camp. The rest of the time was spent with us in agony, experiencing hardship after hardship. I don't know how I survived, or even how my spirit continued to live.

There was one event that I will never forget. We were working on the road, trying to construct it safely. The road had been designed and built by engineers and foremen, but it was our job to insert certain little pieces of wood at given spots, in order to give the highway a straight surface. I hardly knew what I was doing anyway, beyond knowing that it was my job to clear away the dirt that the construction workers had left on the side.

One day I mistakenly covered a certain marker. All of a sudden, the foreman, whose name was Weiman, pounced at me like a raging tiger. When he grew mad, he became the worst sort of a tiger: a tiger who is very hungry. This man walked around killing everyone, literally and figuratively. He beat everybody. When we saw him approaching, it was as if we saw the angel of death.

Weiman had a red face, a mad face, and he was mad at us for more than one reason. First, he was mad at us because we were Jews. Second, he was mad because we didn't know what we were doing. After all, the road crew had taken ordinary young boys, boys who had grown up in yeshivas, and made them work at unskilled labour. And it seemed as if we did everything wrong, leaving Weiman nobody to work with. He really was a master in his work.

Weiman growled his way toward me. And then he paced about, but he couldn't find the marker that I had covered.

"What happened here?" he screamed.

I said in response, "I don't know what happened here."

I tried to be deferential, but it didn't make a difference to him.

He reacted furiously, screaming, "What do you mean you don't know? Don't you see what you did?"

And he went to find something to attack me with, for he was ready to kill me. And I became so afraid. I wasn't afraid that he would shoot me, but I didn't want him to start beating me up like he did to others so often. I was so scared.

He came back. Empty-handed. For some reason, he had changed his mind and walked away from me like a tiger who had lost his hunger and decided not to attack.

As he walked away from me without harming me, I was

sure that I saw the divine hand. And I was alone at that time. All of a sudden he walked away, and I watched as the autumn sun went down.

I reminded myself that it was the eve of Yom Kippur, the Day of Atonement. This was the day that in every other year of my life we went to shul, my family and I. It is the most sacred day of the Jewish year.

I started crying in such a spasmodic way, talking angrily to God. I begged God, saying, "How can you do this? This is the day that we would go to synagogue with our fathers to pray. And now, I am standing here in a strange land, with murderers trying at every moment to kill me, and they enjoy it. *What do you want from us?"*

I kept on crying bitterly. I cried for my mother, my father, and my siblings and friends. I dreaded that I would never see them again. I dreaded the fact that my world was forever changed, and that all Jews were suffering. I wondered where God was.

The next day, I was sick to my stomach from this man, but I still had to work.

Poison Mushrooms

We were constantly transferred from one camp to another in late 1942 and 1943. We were in a camp that was located seventy miles away from Berlin: Neustadt an die Dosse. Here they manufactured ammunition, though one wouldn't have realized this from the appearance of the camp.

The true purpose of the camp was camouflaged from the surface. Above ground, the camp looked like a garden. Underneath, however, poor, sickly Russian inmates worked with gunpowder under the worst of conditions. Many died on the job, just from breathing the gunpowder all day long.

But we were more fortunate. Our transport arrived and we were assigned to work outside. Yet we were starving. We worked for twelve or thirteen hours a day, and were expected to subsist on merely three or four hundred calories a day. When we walked "home" to the barracks each night, some of us couldn't bear the hunger any longer. A few of us simply bent down and tried to eat the grass, though we spat it out right away.

One evening a boy in our group discovered some mushrooms. He looked up at us with desperation, and said, "The heck with it; I'll take a chance and eat them."

This boy died the same night from eating those poison mushrooms. To my shock, his brother and I were ordered to take his body out in a wagon to bury him in the woods. To my horror, workers later cleared out the woods, and they picked his body up ruthlessly with their shovels. Bodies in Nazi camps were given no dignity.

A Sympathetic Story

This short story happened in the agricultural camp where we were prisoners. The *kapo* of the camp was a German (a *kapo* was a prisoner selected to oversee other prisoners). He had originally been an inmate there because he killed somebody and had been thrown into concentration camp. But now, since he was a German, he was appointed overseer of our whole barracks.

I hardly minded this man. He was actually quite a peace-loving person, and he did not seem like a murderer. Even if he had murdered somebody, he was quite human with us. He was especially kind to me because he knew I was a singer.

This episode happened on Christmas night. Because of the holiday, we were given a special ration for bread and salami (we never got salami except on Christmas). It was a very solemn, somber night, especially solemn for the Jewish people. The Christians were very sad, and in general the whole barracks was subdued.

All of a sudden, somebody came over to me and told me that the kapo wanted to see me. Since he was the overseer, I went right away to his quarters—he didn't have a separate room but a separate area in which he lived in the barracks. The kapo said, "I'm feeling very low. Could you sing something to cheer me up a little bit?"

I didn't know what to sing, but I had no choice but to accommodate him. I thought he would be better served if I sang something that wasn't cheerful. So I picked a Yiddish song that actually used the famous melody of *Kol Nidre* (or "All Vows"), the song that we sing on Yom Kippur night, when the tension is great. This special prayer and this special melody are extremely powerful. The melody I sang comes from the Marranos, the Spanish Jews who hid their Jewishness during the Inquisition and the expulsion of the Jews from Spain in the fifteenth century.

And when I finished singing, I witnessed a most moving scene. I have never experienced, anywhere else, how a man of this stature could break down and cry so bitterly. He seemed like a small child. And I myself felt very, very bad. But at the same time I felt elated because my voice had moved him so very much. He began to cry very, very bitterly. I almost regretted that I had sung this particular piece for him. I had pity on him.

He then took half of a loaf of bread and a big chunk of salami. Giving these to me, he said, "Whenever you are hungry, please don't hesitate. Just come over to me and I will always have something for you. I very much appreciate what you did." I will never forget that night.

Sour Soup

Across from our barracks in this same camp lived a French army prisoner-of-war group. They, unlike us, were allowed to receive packages from home. To be kind to those of us who were less fortunate, they threw their soup rations into a big barrel each day, and sometimes we were able to dig into it. The contents of this barrel could have been a week old.

We knew the soup wasn't healthy, but some of us were so hungry that we couldn't restrain ourselves.

One day, a boy from our barracks risked his life and climbed over the fence to steal some of the rotting soup. He looked around, saw that no guard was looking, and was able to retrieve a bowl of soup.

But he was wrong in thinking that no guard had observed him. Right when he went back over the fence, the Nazi guards shot and killed him on the spot.

This episode happened in front of my eyes. How sad it was that this poor boy thought he was lucky but was shot to death over a bowl of sour soup that had probably been sitting for a week in the sun.

### Kreutze: An Even More Brutal Camp

Another camp, called Kreutze, was located next to our camp. It was almost impossible for me to believe, but this wretched place offered its residents even worse conditions than we ourselves experienced.

Because Kreutze was right next to the area where we worked, we sometimes could talk to the people who had been sentenced to live there. They were not far from us. They worked in a different area but did the same type of work. However, those unfortunate people worked many hours longer than we did. They were given even less food to eat than we received. And they always had the misfortune of being watched over by a *Lagerführer*, or director in charge of the camp, who was a terrible anti-Semite as well as a terrible womanizer.

Their Lagerführer tried to keep all of the camp's money for himself. When he was given a new budget by the authorities, he tried to hold on to the surplus funds and thought his workers would get by if they would eat less and work harder.

Those people were beaten every single day. They told us stories that even we couldn't believe. But we *had* to believe them because we saw the way they looked. Some of them were bloody, and all of them had wounds covering their bodies. Scores of them were beaten to death every single day, and those who survived didn't receive even meagre rations to eat.

Among them was a young man who must have been twenty-five or twenty-six years old—older than me but still young. He was a fine singer: not a cantor or a professional, but a beautiful singer nonetheless. One day we asked him to sing something for us. In response, he sang so beautifully that if someone heard him today, he would win stipends and scholarships, gold and silver. But when he finished singing in the camp, it was very noticeable to us that he didn't have any energy left. Unfortunately, I don't think this boy lived very long, since he was very run down, in terrible condition.

Our Chance to Return to the Ghetto

The camp was endlessly brutal and terrifying. But one day a surprise announcement produced an inkling of hope for many of us. The booming voice of the camp commandant suddenly made us dream that we could go home. "Whoever wants to go back to the ghetto is free to do so," came the call. "If you wish to leave the camp to return to where you came from, you must register your names now."

What were we to do? Nobody seemed to know how to respond. Was this just another tantalizing game? And even if we did return "home," what would we find there? Would I see my beloved mother and father, my brothers and sisters again? We were so confused, so torn about what we might find.

We consulted with the camp doctor. He was a Jewish man who was married to a German gentile woman, and for some reason the Germans treated him a little better than they treated most of us Jews. My brother and I were on very good terms with this doctor, and we thought he might have some inside information about the offer to let us go back to the ghetto.

"Should we register to go home?" we asked him.

A horrible look came across his face. "Don't you dare leave," he whispered back to us.

"Why?" we pleaded with him.

"I'm not at liberty to tell you what I know," he answered. "And I don't know if what I know is true, but I *beg* you, please don't go. Stay put. It isn't good here, but I beg you not to take your chances. Don't register."

And we listened to him. We didn't go. We trusted the tone that we had heard in his voice.

But many other people did leave. And one day we came home and heard of the fate of the people who had registered. A van had come to take them "home." No, it wasn't really a van; it was more like a closed bus. The Nazis closed the door of this green bus, packing in around ninety people, all of whom had registered.

These unfortunate people were gassed five minutes later. When we came back from work, we were informed about it.

Among those people who were gassed on the bus was a young man whose last name was Feder. He was a brother of my brother's sister-in-law. When I came to Montreal years later, I heard the surname Feder again; it was the name of a rabbi who was teaching at Herzliah High School. Rabbi Feder knew that his brother hadn't survived, but I asked him if he had ever found out how his brother had really died. "Do you know what happened to him?" I asked, not sure if I should proceed with my answer. Sometimes it is better for people not to know the truth. But he wanted to know. And when I told him, he grew terribly upset, even though he knew that his brother had died.

Later on, when we left this camp and were en route to another camp not far from Berlin, we met the inmates of Kreutze once again. They shared our transport, and we could see that their physical conditions were simply horrible. They had declined to the point that they were hardly recognizable as human beings. Horrible, and yet again horrible. We couldn't understand—I still cannot understand—how people could treat other people like this, with such force, with such hatred. The Germans were real beasts, and there were very few who didn't act in this manner. They were beasts, they were the most loathsome animals humanity could imagine. In fact, they were *worse* than animals, because animals can't create crematoriums. And these so-called human beings *did* make crematoriums.

### Yet Another Camp

Freight trains were waiting for us. We must have numbered about four hundred people, and they packed us in, though in fact we were not terribly cramped. And then they locked the train wagons from the outside so that no one could escape. We had no idea about where we were going.

After a whole night and a day, we were let out of the trains. How did we feel? We couldn't recognize each other because we had been in wagons that had previously been used for transporting coal. We were all filthy, as if our exposed skins had been painted with soot. The images that we received of each other were so unreal that we just laughed and cried together. Most of all, we were terribly hungry. We really didn't care how we looked.

We were led into a big dining room, where they had prepared soup for us. And this time, to our amazement, the head of the camp, the Lagerführer, was a very nice man. He made sure that we were served a nourishing soup. The cooks were French prisoners of war who were assigned to the kitchen.

This camp was not far from Berlin, near Neustadt on the Dosse. It was called Dretz, and it was smaller than most of the other camps.

We worked hard, as usual. We became builders. The real work, however, was done by the Russians, who were located underground in the ammunition factory. From above ground, nobody could notice what the real work was about, because the land was camouflaged as a garden. But underneath were factories where the Russian prisoners worked with gunpowder. These workers looked awful. Being underground all the time, working with gunpowder, gave them a sickly appearance. Most of them did not last long.

We were assigned the task of building a new section of the underground factories. My job was to cut with a saw, to measure the board and wood for the building. One day as I stood working, I cut two of my fingers severely. Two fingers were just hanging by a hair. It was painful, but in reality, this event was my lucky break. For six weeks afterward, I couldn't work.

The doctor was a half Jew, and he said, "If I hadn't known you were a singer, and that one day you might really be singing on the stage, I would cut off the two fingers because it doesn't pay to preserve them. But since you are going to have to work as a carpenter, I'll try to fix them."

This was my break in this camp. Others weren't so lucky: it was in this camp that the starvation was so prevalent. If somebody stole just a little soup, they got shot for it.

# *Auschwitz-Birkenau: Arbeit Macht Frei*

After I had worked for a year in the ammunition camp, we heard a rumour that we soon would be transferred to another camp. Sure enough, a few days later, Germans in civilian clothes came and told us that we were being transferred to a work camp. With their inhuman voices, they announced that we should prepare ourselves to leave. Some of us were very happy, some not. The people who did not wish to leave were afraid to tamper with the status quo; they worried that things would be even worse in the new camp. But others of us were hungry above anything else, and we thought that the situations could not be worse elsewhere. Maybe in the new camp there would be more food; maybe it was a better camp.

The day came. They herded us into the usual transportation,

the train. Wagons waited for us, and two hundred of us were crowded into the cars, as if we were mere cattle. We traveled all night, not knowing where we were going. We couldn't even ascertain the direction that the train was traveling. Guards surrounded us and we were not allowed to question them.

The next day, the train came to a halt and we were ordered to get down. Accompanied by the usual yelling and shrieking of the Germans, we followed our orders. They shrieked, "*Schneller! Schneller!* Faster! Faster!" And so we marched.

Soon we were shoved before a big iron gate with the now-famous sign, *Arbeit macht Frei:* "Work will set you free." We hadn't ever heard anything about Auschwitz or Birkenau. And this was Birkenau, the worst camp of all. Here we were to encounter the crematoriums.

As we walked in, we were met by vicious-looking Jews with military-style armbands. They represented a kind of concentration camp police. Carrying big sticks and aiming them at whomever they wanted, they started beating us with the sticks. We were stunned. We didn't know why. We didn't understand what was happening to us. One of us pleaded with them, crying, "Tell me why. You are Jewish. And I am Jewish. You don't know me. We came just now. Why are you hitting us? Why are you beating us?"

The response was a shock. The man to whom we pleaded started beating us even harder.

Then he screamed back at us, "Why should I have pity on you? In this camp, we watch how people are being beaten to death. Thousands are being burned. So what do you want? Do you think you have come to a hotel?"

After we marched in, they took us to a horrific barracks. Within it there was a long oven, like in a bakery. We were ordered to lie down on the dirt floor. We were ordered to lie down and nobody was even allowed to lift his head. If someone did, he regretted it very much.

Next, one of the same guards who had met us at the gate

gave us a speech. He walked back and forth in this oven and told us the following, without a trace of sympathy or pity in his voice: "In order that you know why you are here, I have to tell you that this place is called Birkenau. In this place, we have four crematoriums. The fifth one is being built."

He went on: "Whatever you have, you must surrender to us now. If you have a gold watch or a ring, or even photographs from home, you must give them up. Anything, everything. I want to see everything you own put on this table. And it will be very bad for you if you do not obey this order. If you are going to spend three or four days here, you will be very strong men, and for you to learn where you are, you had better put everything on this table."

A man in his forties started to feel ill. He lifted his head because his pain was so bad. In response, the guard rushed over to him. The guard gave him such a bang over his head that he never got up.

I was lying, crouched on the floor, with my brother Mayer next to me. We were together and we both carefully considered the next words of the guard: "If you want to make it easy for yourself, we have an electric fence here. If you prefer to be electrocuted, you can do so. It will be less painful. So you have your choice: either the ovens or the electric fence."

My brother whispered that he thought the electric fence might be a good idea. Maybe we should kill ourselves on our own, he thought. We should try to run away.

I replied, "No. Never. I will never throw myself onto an electric fence. Let's not think about this."

And being religious, I davened, prayed by heart, because I knew my prayers so well. It was the time of day to pray the evening service, and it was also the time of year when for seven weeks between Passover and Shavuot (the Feast of Weeks, commemorating the giving of the Torah at Sinai) we counted the *Omer* (an offering for the Temple), which meant reciting a special prayer. As I lay on the floor, I just started praying to myself quietly.

And I even remember which day it was; it was late May, two or three days before the holiday of Shavuot.

When I finished praying, I told my brother again that I didn't want to die on the electric fence. Something told me—I don't know what, but something told me—that I didn't think that we were going to remain in Birkenau. I felt that we shouldn't give up hope. We lay there all night, unable to sleep, even though we were exhausted, even though we had just heard of the worst horrors that could be dealt to humanity.

Sure enough, in the morning a high ranking SS officer came in, looking like the Angel of Death with his severe special hat and special medals. He stomped his way over and he asked the Jewish kapos, "How many *Juden,* how many Jews do you have here?"

The kapo replied, "We have two hundred."

"Where did they come here from?"

He was told that we had come from another camp, to which the SS officer responded, "Then these are people who are used to working. They need to be put to work. I want the whole group to get to Auschwitz. Give them coffee and get them ready."

We had never heard of Auschwitz, but we heard that we were going to work and that we were getting out of this hell. One night alone in this Birkenau: this one night had been hell on earth. It had hit us hard, in a terrible, terrible way from the moment that we had entered it.

And so we started marching. We marched from Birkenau to Auschwitz, which wasn't a long distance. We came there and they immediately mutilated us, tatooing numbers on our arms. A Russian inmate was skilled at imprinting us. It was painful, pricking.

And we took a shower. They didn't give us towels, and we had to dry outside. It wasn't too warm yet. Nevertheless we were very very happy that we were no longer in Birkenau, in hell.

The very next day, something happened to my brother and me that I will never forget in my whole life. They ordered us again, using the word *Antreten*, which means to form a column with rows five men across. They took a hundred of us, and made us stand one next to one another. To our miserable disappointment, they wanted two columns of fifty and fifty. The SS were there and they divided us into groups of ten times five; fifty of us were to go to one camp, and the other fifty to another camp.

To my shock, my brother was separated from me and was forced into the other column. I moaned in fright, "What will happen? If we are separated, we will never see each other again."

And he started weeping, and I started crying spasmodically. We forgot about our hunger, we forgot about everything, and we couldn't even eat. We were choking.

The SS officers announced that in the afternoon, two hours from then, we would have to stand again in the same formation, fifty and fifty. At that point we would inevitably be separated forever. I didn't care what happened. I took my brother and brought him to my column. And when they came and counted our numbers, there were forty-nine in one column and fifty-one in the other.

Furious, the SS man, an officer of high rank, came over and shrieked threateningly, "Who was here who should be in the other column?"

My brother and I didn't say anything, but there was one Jew who wanted to be wise, to get a good name perhaps. He pointed to my brother and said, "This is the one." The officer fiercely took my brother out of line and asked him why he had disobeyed the orders. He asked him quietly, even very nicely.

My brother didn't answer, so I stepped forward and said, "He is my brother." I spoke in German, which I could speak quite well at that time. "He is my brother and if we are separated, I know I will never see him again. I don't want to be separated from him. I hope you understand."

The officer looked at me and slowly put his hand to his gun. He pulled out the gun, cursing, "You *Jude verfluchte,* you miserable, cursed Jew. I am going to shoot you like a dog right here." His voice grew louder and louder. But I didn't react. I didn't even bat an eyelash. I didn't say anything except, "*Bitte.* Please. So be it if you want."

For me it wasn't such a big thing to die. Too much of me had died already. I knew that we couldn't survive for long in that hell, so rather than be separated, I agreed to be shot. But then, slowly, slowly, as if an angel had come down to direct his hands, the officer put his gun back. But then he took my brother and smashed him with force, sending him to the other group. We were separated, then, but we still saw each other. Mayer was not stationed far away.

It happened that one day I went to work at an agricultural establishment three kilometres from Auschwitz; this farm camp was called Babitz. It was an agricultural camp, with cows and horses that were treated with more respect that the workers. My brother, I found out, had been sent nearby to Buna, the I. G. Farben Industry camp. He worked for them. It happened later, when I was given a more prominent position in the camp as a *Magaziner*, or inventory manager for the camp, that I was able to ask the SS commander to let me see my brother who was working in a certain field. To my joy, a guard was allowed to accompany me to visit him. I was able to bring some bread and gifts to him.

# A Strange Symphony

At Babitz I had some fortunate breaks. When I arrived, they asked the members of our group to announce our skills and professions. I didn't want to say anything, but someone from Lodz told the camp commanders that I was a singer.

The next morning, I was sent out into the field to work. I watched a group of Russians marching with scythes on their shoulders, and I was sent to join this group. I protested, however. I said, "I don't know how to do anything. I was never a farmer and I don't know how to cut grass or corn."

The officer who ordered me around replied, "You're not going to cut grass. Just take a rake." So I took the rake on my shoulders just like they did, and we started marching. They started singing; the Russians were always singing when they went out to march. We came to a place where we were supposed to cut the high grass, to clean the field. The area was filled with stones, and we were ordered to remove them.

Two people were required to transport platforms to gather the stones, and they had to do this while running across the field. They had no time to complain or to protest. There was a stone, a huge rock in the field, taller than two people, that seemed to have been there from the beginning of time.

To my absurd amazement, the SS man asked me to climb up on the stone to sing, since he had heard of my talent. He himself was a rather intelligent person who appreciated music. When I was at the top of the rock, I asked him, "What would you like me to sing?"

He replied, "Anything you want. Sing in German."

I knew a few songs by Schubert, and *O Tannenbaum* for Christmas, so I started singing. My voice had lost some of its power because I was quite starved by then (I must have weighed no more than 120 pounds), but I started singing. When I stopped, the man said, "You will sing. Don't stop."

I was singing and the workers were being beaten because they were not fast enough, and the guards were yelling and yelling. It was a symphony that one cannot imagine unless one was there. Otherwise it was indescribable, absolutely indescribable. Finally, I ran out of German songs to sing. Out of desperation, I started singing Yiddish songs. The officer happened to like this.

"More, more," he demanded.

I sang for about five hours until my throat was so dry that I couldn't sing any longer. Then the officer brought me a little apple, green and sour and almost impossible to eat. Nevertheless, I ate it (and felt sick later), because it brought a little moisture to my throat.

The next day this officer expressed his pleasure about my "concert." He told the other man in charge that I should work in the *Magazin*, the store, since he considered me to be an intelligent man. He asked if I could write in German, and I said definitely, I do. I didn't need to have the skill of a lawyer to write down how many shovels and how many picks or rakes were in stock. Let me explain the meaning of *Magaziner.* In German, it is a place where they file away tools and machinery, and everything else that is needed for the people to go out to work. Workers couldn't work with their bare hands. Therefore, a group cutting the grass got scythes. Those who dug dirt got shovels. Some needed picks and some needed rakes. These were stored away in a Magazin. While I was in charge of this, they called me "Magaziner." Thus I had a break at this camp. Undoubtedly, my voice saved my life.

My strange concert took place in 1943. And I was able to work in the Magazin for a while.

# The Unfortunate Greeks

Before the Hungarians came in 1944, there was a mixture of many nationalities in our barracks. There were Jews and non-Jews. There were Czechs, there were Germans, there were Russians, and there were Greeks from Salonika. The Greeks were treated very, very badly because they couldn't speak the language. They didn't understand one word the guards said. And the guards had no patience for this. When they gave an order, they expected a response right away, and if the person didn't understand, it was too bad.

The SS ordered a Greek man to do something. Unfortunately, the man didn't comprehend what he had been asked to do. In response, the guards squeezed his testicles. They knew this was very painful. And this man was in such agony, yelling so loudly, that it seemed as if he could be heard a mile away.

Someone asked the guard, "How can you do this to a human

being? After all, you are human too. And the man didn't understand what you were asking him to do. If he had understood you, he would have listened to you."

The guard looked at him with total disdain, saying, "Who asked you!?" And he started beating up the man who had dared to ask the question, worse than he had beaten the other one. We were standing there but there was nothing that we could do, short of killing the guard by ourselves. And had we done that, then at least ten of us would have been shot immediately.

Yes, that is true. If one Jew did something "wrong," then the SS took ten, or twenty, or twenty-five other Jews, and they shot them right on the spot. They took our lives just at will. And there were many, many other happenings, too numerous to mention. In other words, there was misery, there was starvation, and there was simple doom.

There was one time when we were standing outside, and we saw very tiny airplanes above us in the sky. They were probably on bombing missions to a nearby area, the big cities. But we were standing and praying like one who is thirsty, like one who wants a little rain to swallow. This is how we looked up, but we were not looking up in joy. No: we wanted and prayed only to be killed. We prayed for them to drop a bomb on us, a few bombs to finish us off. I remember that every single night, when I went to bed as a religious person reciting the *Shma* (the "Hear, O Israel" prayer). But now this is how I prayed: that I should never get up in the morning. And I was not the biggest pessimist. There were others who were even worse. Even I believed that somehow maybe we would be rescued. Nevertheless, I prayed that we would be killed, that I would never again wake up in the morning to live through what we lived through for so many years.

# *Together with the Hungarian Jews*

One morning in 1944, all the non-Jewish nationalities were suddenly removed from our barracks. There were around two hundred of us, each with only a bed. After the others—the Russians, Poles, German criminals, and Czechs—marched out, there were just us forty Jews remaining. We thought for sure that they were now going to finish us off.

To our astonishment, however, the gates suddenly opened and 160 Hungarian Jews marched in from a transport. We welcomed them and were happy that we would be all Jews together. The only non-Jew among us was a Pole, who was in charge of us. One Pole, and he had his special quarters for living. Besides him there was just us Jews.

The first or second morning after this event, I was in my

Magazin, keeping control of the stock. As I wrote down the figures, I heard someone praying and crying, praying and crying behind the walls. I went out to see who it was, and learned that the voice belonged to a rabbi from a town not far from Budapest. He was the grandson of a great sage from Sighet. He was a very fragile man, and he was praying, reciting psalms while he cleaned up and performed his duties.

I came out and told him not to cry. I assured him that we would have a minyan on the high holidays. He looked at me incredulously, with astonishment. How could we possibly think that we would still be there in this camp that far in the future? The holidays were still three months away!

He assured me then, with a confidence that I had long ago lost: God would help us and we would be long liberated. And I thought, from your mouth to God's ears. I said, "All right, all right, let's hope that it will be as you say."

And I convinced the *Kommandoführer* (the person in charge of a work team) to allow the rabbi to work with me in my Magazin all the time. I felt that otherwise he would be killed. A man like him didn't know how to hold a shovel in his hand. And sure enough, this was a miserable Kommandoführer, a Ukrainian. He was a short little guy who took pleasure in beating people until they couldn't get up anymore. This miserable creature beat up one man, the bookkeeper, an intelligent man. The bookkeeper was Jewish but he had a German wife. One day the bookkeeper had opened his mouth a little too much, and had been thrown into concentration camp.

The Ukrainian Kommandoführer took particular pleasure in beating him up. He knew he couldn't beat him to death, but he beat him up just for his pleasure. When I saw this, I felt like just losing myself. Rage enveloped me, and I was tempted to take whatever I had in my hands and knock the guard down to the ground. And something important happened. If the people who witnessed it are still alive, they will bear me out. I know one went to Israel but I don't know where he is.

We were all Jews, and we tried to make a minyan, ten people to perform a service. We had more than that; half the camp were religious Jews. So we had some sort of autonomy, and the kapo Konrad didn't like it. He knew I was a little higher up than the other inmates because I was the Magaziner, and I was responsible only to the director, the *Oberscharführer*, who was an SS but a very intelligent man.

The director was a very intelligent man who knew exactly what he was doing. He was an SS but he didn't act like one, especially when he would come into my Magazin, the stock-inventory barracks where I worked. Each time this man came over, he would ask me, "What's new? Do you need me to bring you anything from Auschwitz?"

Everything was sent over to us from Auschwitz, even our food. Every day. With this in mind, he would inquire of me, "Do you need any more shovels? Do you need any scythes? If something isn't good anymore, write it down and give me a report and I'll get you new supplies."

I was very diligent in my work. I did everything properly. He became very friendly with me in a way that was not usual for a high-ranking SS. It was not an ordinary thing for a member of the SS to be friendly with a Jew who was an inmate. But that is exactly what happened with us.

One evening I came back to the sleeping barracks later than all of the other inmates. This wasn't unusual: I would arrive after everyone because it was my job to see that all the tools were placed back where they belonged. I also would separate the tools that had to be cleaned. On this particular evening, I entered the barracks, looking for my soap. Suddenly Konrad the kapo called me over and told me to come into his quarters. He said, "Do you know why I have called you here?"

His voice was vicious. He was a malicious person who pretended that he was a bigshot who had dealings with the

Kommandoführer, the little Ukrainian. But more than anything, he took pleasure in beating up people.

I replied, "No. I have no idea why you have called me. What is it that you want?" In response, he gave me two slaps across my face. His slap knocked down my glasses and broke one of the lenses. Somehow I managed to blurt out a reply to him. "Listen, Konrad," I said in Polish. "I know that you are stronger than me, and I'm not going to fight with you or hit you back. But I think you will regret what you just did."

He slapped me again, of course, and sent me back to my quarters. It turned out that I was being punished for having placed a piece of bread under my thin mattress. This act was a sin. I had wanted to save the bread for later in the day, but apparently this was forbidden.

I stumbled back to my bed in pain, with my glasses broken. The same evening, a young boy joined us in the barracks. He was known as a *Kalfactor*, which meant that he acted like a personal slave to the Oberscharführer, the man in charge of everything in the camp. This boy would shine the Oberscharfuhrer's shoes, and he brought him milk and anything else that was demanded.

Where was this boy from? There were ten or twelve boys like him from Lodz. They were actually older than mere boys, but since they were undernourished, they looked much younger than they actually were. This particular boy was so beautiful looking. They had especially chosen the good-looking ones to do this work, to be the slaves of the SS. They were the slaves of the bigshots.

I knew this boy, and I called him over to see if he could help me. "Would you do me a favour," I asked him gently.

He nodded his head. "Could you go to the Oberscharfuhrer, the one in charge, and tell him that I *have* to talk to him? Please, when you bring him his milk in the morning, please tell him that the Magaziner wants to tell him something important…"

An ad from a Lodz Ghetto newspaper announcing Solomon Gisser's appearance in a VIP soup kitchen during the High Holy Days in 1940.

Solomon Gisser in 1950, before leaving Europe for Canada.

The Shaare Zion Synagogue in Montreal, Canada, where Solomon Gisser served as Cantor for 45 years.

Solomon Gisser in 1976.

Solomon Gisser in 1977, on the occasion of his 25th Anniversary as the Cantor at Shaare Zion.

Cantor Gisser receives an Honorary Fellowship from Vice Chancellor Dr. Mandelbaum of the Jewish Theological Seminary.

Solomon Gisser in 1997, upon his retirement from his position as Cantor at the Shaare Zion Synagogue in Montreal.

The next morning I went to my Magazin as usual. Shortly after I got there, the Oberscharführer entered the premises on his horse. He looked quite imposing with a large whip in his hand. Slowly he came off on the horse's back, and entered the Magazin where I was waiting to greet him. "What can I do?" he asked with genuine interest. "What is the matter?"

I looked at him gravely. Slowly I said, "What I have to tell you is very regrettable. And I really don't like to be an informer, but I just can't let things go on the way they have been anymore."

He then asked me with concern, "What is it?" Looking carefully at me, he also asked, "By the way, where are your glasses?" He had seen that I had just one glass lens in the frame. He repeated, "What happened to your lens?"

I said, "I'll tell you the whole story." I continued, with a sense of desperation in my voice. "When I came back to the barracks last night, I was mercilessly beaten by Konrad. He can't stand Jews. He doesn't like us. I came in and he started slapping me around for no reason at all. And now I know that it can only get worse, because he really feels like a king around all the Jews. And he thinks that he's a big shot because he has dealings with the Kommanderführer. But he's a little guy who is a murderer."

I took a breath and added what I had been waiting to say: "The men come back to the barracks every night from work. They work very hard and try to do their best, but every day he beats up someone else. He takes pleasure in showing his authority. But for your information, I want you to know that this guy has all kinds of deals going with the Kommandoführer. When we go to bed, he goes to the fence and buys liquor from the Poles. In turn, he gives them the shoes and clothes that you really got for us so that we would be able to work. He takes the good stuff and both of them are selling it to the people, the Poles, behind the fence."

The Oberscharführer looked shocked. In reply, he stated,

"Oh, this is very interesting. I want to see him immediately. Can you send him over to me now?" I said, "Yes." And I felt a sinister pleasure rising in my heart. Konrad was only about ten meters away, sitting in his domain like a prince. I went over and said to him, "Konrad, the Oberscharführer wants to speak to you."

When Konrad soon sauntered over, the Oberscharführer literally threw him against the wall. "What am I hearing about you? Why did you beat up my Magaziner?" Konrad replied, "I found a piece of bread under his mattress."

"For this do you have to break his glasses?" His voice grew sterner. "And now something else. What do you have to do with the Kommandoführer? What have you done with the shoes and the clothes that I bring to the men in your barracks?"

Even before he received an answer, the Oberscharführer whipped Konrad across the face with the whip that he used for the horse: back and forth, back and forth. And each time that Konrad fell down, the Oberscharführer screamed, "Get up! Why did you do this? Why did you do this?" Then he said, "You are going to regret what you have done. The people who are here have come to work. You have no jurisdiction over them to beat them up." He called four guards then, to come in and to escort Konrad out of the camp area. They took him to Auschwitz, where there was a jail. They put him there.

That same evening, some of my close friends were angry at me. They said with fear in their voices, "Why did you do this? Don't you know that this Kommandoführer will get back to you and kill you for sure? Why did you do this? Do you know what situation you have gotten yourself into now? Do you know the danger you have placed yourself in?"

I said, "I don't care. I had to do it, and I hope that the Oberscharführer has a higher rank than the Kommandoführer. Let him go to hell. I don't care. If he kills me, he will kill me, and there will be one less Jew. But I had to do it."

I still remember the name of two of the young men who were particularly worried about me. One was a skillful watchmaker named Heinrich; because of his skills he helped to repair tools in the camp. He could fix trucks, and he knew everything about being a handyman. He was also a very religious boy. I hope he is still alive in Israel.

And there was another intelligent young man, named Millstein. Both of them kept telling me, "We are very worried about you."

They were right in worrying about me. That very same evening, the doors opened and somehow Konrad had returned. I was sitting in the barracks, wearing my hat. And as soon as he entered the room, he came over to me and said mockingly, "Why do you have your hat on? Don't you understand that you don't need it? You're not supposed to have your hat on." He took it off my head and threw it across the room. I went over to where he had thrown the hat and put it back onto my head again. I turned to him and said with strength in my voice, "You have nothing more to say here. I don't think you belong here."

Something must have gone wrong in the jail at Auschwitz. Perhaps they didn't have space for him. In any event, something went sour. But I soon got some relief from this situation. Not even ten minutes later, the Oberscharführer came in, saw who was there, and said with amazement to Konrad, "What! You've come back?"

The Oberscharführer started yelling at the guards, commanding, "Remove him immediately! Remove him immediately!" They took Konrad out. Later on, I heard that he had been wounded when a bomb exploded near him. He got his right hand cut by shrapnel.

But this was not all. Even though the Oberscharführer might have dealt fairly with me, I still had to face the Kommandoführer, who came in the next morning and said sneakily to me, "Konrad got what he deserved, but I'm not yet done with you." I didn't say a thing right then. But I had thought of a strategy for dealing with him, and I knew that the strategy was going to work. I knew that the Kommandoführer, the little Ukrainian, liked women terribly, so I said to him at some point, while pretending to be grimacing in pain, "I have a toothache. I have to go to Auschwitz." That's where they treated dental problems.

So they took me over to Auschwitz on the wagon that brought us our food everyday. They used this wagon to take people back and forth from the infirmary at Auschwitz.

For my excursion to Auschwitz, I had saved up some bread. There I was able to barter the bread for nylon stockings that were constantly found in the packages that poor Jews brought with them during their transports. After these Jews were sent to the crematorium, their goods were confiscated.

These doomed people had brought packages with all kinds of valuable items hidden in them. The SS guards would ask us to cut open the bread to see if something was hidden in it. Some found diamond rings; I once found a beautiful gold watch, the kind that a groom would receive upon his marriage. And I had to give it away because we couldn't keep what we found.

But on this particular day, I was able to barter my bread for several pairs of nylon stockings. When I returned to my barracks, I said to the Kommanderführer, "Here, I know that you need some stockings."

Amazingly, he shut his mouth. And I never had another thing to do with him. He was afraid of me like I was afraid of fire. He knew that if I had snitched on him once, I could do it again. And he was afraid to beat me up and certainly to shoot me, because he knew that the overseer would punish him in turn.

I was very proud of the way I handled myself in this incident. I will never forget the whole scene; indeed, in front of my eyes I can still envision every event that happened over that two-day period.

# Unbelievable Tales of Escape

One day, the Nazis brought in a tall Russian prisoner of war to my Magazin. They brought him in, led by two guards, and they tied him down to a pole. In the Magazin, each section of tools was separated from the others by a pole. They tied the prisoner down there, and started beating him and kicking him with their boots. I couldn't understand how he lived after one such kick from their boots. Other guards came in to stare at him and kick him too. The Russian prisoner apparently had tried to run away.

They kicked him and they beat him. They left and I was there with another Russian, who was a blacksmith working near the door so that he would have enough light. When the guards left, we tried to help the prisoner, to give him something, but he was almost dead. The beating had been unbelievable. He was in his shirt. So we didn't know what happened, why exactly he was there. I asked one of the guards of the post, "Why did you bring him in? What happened here?"

He replied, "We found him outside with a motorbike. He pretended that he was bringing it for another SS, another Kommanderführer, just to be helpful, to bring him a bike like they sometimes do. But he didn't know how the bike worked, and he fell down. Then he started it again, and he wanted it to run, but he fell down again. The post sounded an alarm, on the tower; so they caught him and brought him back to the Magazin."

He was a young man, probably in his twenties, twenty-six, twenty-seven, a tall Russian fellow. We couldn't help him very much. He was tied down, and we tried to give him a little water. He was out, unconscious. So we thought he was nearly finished, dead. We had already seen many people who were being beaten to death. We saw it often: I, too many times with my own eyes. Although it was almost routine for me to see such scenes, this was nevertheless a different case. I was talking to the smith, to the Russian fellow, and talking to him about cruelty, and how the Nazis could do this. All of a sudden, the smith screamed out to me, "Look! Look!"

I turned around. The Russian prisoner had managed to get up, even though he had been tied down there, amid the scythes to cut the corn, to cut the grass. He managed to get up, and then in horror we watched as he purposely cut his throat in front of our eyes. He cut his throat half through. His blood was all over. But he wanted to die, to make an end to his whole life, because he knew the fate that was awaiting him.

I will never forget this whole spectacle. He had the courage to pick up the scythe, to pick himself up from the ropes, and to get up and cut his throat. He died immediately. He had the courage and the strength to kill himself.

There were other events in this camp too which ended on a happier note. There was a Polish veterinarian, in charge of the animals. In the middle of the night, he was called because a horse had become sick. The guards noticed that the horse was very wild in its stable, and they had to call the doctor to help. He knew what was going to happen because in reality he had already given the horse a certain medicine to become wild. He knew. He had everything prepared, and they called him. He sent a guard to bring something for the horse, and they ran to bring it to the animal.

While they were running away, the veterinarian grabbed scissors, special ones capable of cutting the fence, and he cut a hole and ran away. Later, the SS pretended they caught him, but we knew that he was never really caught. For us, this action represented a real triumph. They had said that nobody could escape from this camp. But he ran away, in a very beautiful way. His escape was very clean: he just made a hole and ran away.

People said, "Naturally it couldn't have happened for a Jew. A Pollack has his friends." Jews didn't have any friends. If he had been a Jew, he wouldn't have succeeded; he never would have gotten away.

And there is another little story that took place in Auschwitz, in the camp that we called Babitz, the agricultural camp. One evening, we heard the order to Antreten, which meant that we were to stand in formation so that they could count us. This was a nightly ritual for the SS.

On this particular evening, one man was missing. The SS yelled out, "Who is missing? Does anybody know him?"

Nobody answered. Nobody knew. Or nobody would admit the answer. Finally they decided to start inspecting us while we stood there. They wouldn't let us into the barracks until they found the missing man. All the guards started looking, until they suspected that the person was hiding in a barn, where there were piles of hay and straw.

The man who had escaped was a young Russian. He thought that after dark he would somehow be able to slip out of the barracks. The guards looked and looked and looked, all over the barn. They suspected that he was hiding there, because one of the doors was not locked. And sure enough, they found him up high, waiting very quietly on a ball of hay. And the SS took him. They brutally led him to a little window very high up. They threw him out the window and he was killed instantly, mercilessly.

We were watching. We watched how he died right on the spot. This killing was performed by one of the German and one of the Ukrainian guards. They were the worst guards of all.

# *Leaving Auschwitz: The Death March*

It was on the 18th of January 1945 when the command came for us to leave Auschwitz. The Germans suddenly became wild because they had heard that the Russians were not too far away. The Germans started yelling and rushing us out of the camp. The SS acted like wild beasts as they hollered, "*Schnell, schnell*, get out!"

As we marched out of the camp, we saw a big fire. Flames and smoke rose into the sky. No, it was not a military attack. No, Jews were not being burned this time. Instead, the Nazis were burning documents, burning papers. Burning the evidence of our humiliation.

We walked out into the darkening night. We didn't know where we were expected to go. Some of us wanted to hide.

We knew that if we were successful at hiding, the Germans would march out, far away from us, and that the Russians would come and we would be free.

At first, I decided to hide too. I left the group and went back to my Magazin. I hid in a little corner. But it didn't feel right. As I stood there, my heart was pounding at what seemed like a million times a minute. But then, all of a sudden, something came upon me, and I said, "If my destiny really is to live, then maybe I shouldn't take such a chance."

So I came out and started mixing with the others. And we started marching and marching. We marched on and on—Elie Wiesel was among our group, and he describes the march in his novels and memoirs—and it was already night and bitter cold. Remember, it was still the middle of January. We were not dressed for the cold winter climate. All I had was a miserable blanket that wasn't very warm.

As it grew darker, a grim announcement came from our enslavers. They screamed out that whoever didn't walk *schnell* enough (fast enough), and whoever dared to stay behind, would be shot on the spot. And it seemed that every thirty seconds I would hear a shot. Sure enough, just about every two meters along the route I could spy a dead body, pierced by a bullet, lying in a ditch.

And they were yelling and we were marching and marching, at night. It was an unbelievable scene. The high-ups were on horses and motor bikes, yelling, "*Schnell*!" They pressed us to move quickly, yelling "Get out of here *schnell!!!* Out of here quick!" They didn't want the Russians to catch us. We knew too much; we held too much evidence.

We might have been marching to freedom, but we were still their hostages. We marched and marched the whole night long, and so many hundreds of us were shot. It was a scene that one can only imagine in a dream when one dreams about hell. No, when one dreams about hell and wants to imagine what hell is, this was ten times hell. And we were hungry, starving. They gave us nothing to eat, not anything, and it was bitter cold. Fortunately, I was younger and relatively healthy. The elderly ones who couldn't walk fast were shot right on the spot.

Eventually, another sadistic voice told us to stop marching. It was the middle of the night, and we had apparently arrived at a farm. The Germans marched us straight into a barn. The barn was full of straw and hay. Still it was a shelter of sorts. We arrived so exhausted that we fell asleep almost at once. We fell down on the ground and took what sleep we could. We were the lucky ones. Other people were locked into barns that the Nazis then burned down. We were lucky that they allowed us to make it through the night.

The next morning, they woke us up again with their brutal shouting. We walked a little longer until we came to a place where they let us board wagons. Again we were lucky: these wagons were open rather than closed. Those people who were pushed into the closed wagons died because they had no water, they had no air. They had nothing, and we were lucky that ours were open.

It was snowing the next day. But for us, the snow was like an oasis. Each of us had a spoon, so we scooped off the snow from each other's backs. I will never forget how heavenly the snow tasted in my mouth. We were hungry, we were so thirsty. There was no water, and no food, so we drank snow.

Finally we arrived at Buchenwald. The camp was crowded way beyond its capacity. There were 120,000 inmates squeezed into an unhealthy, filthy area. There were 2,000 men in a barracks that had been built for only 500.

The Germans couldn't bring in our food or the kettles for cooking it, because there was no space. Instead, they gave us tickets to go to a movie house every day, where we would pick up our barely edible meals. We got a ticket once a day, entitling us to a meal that couldn't have provided us with more than 200 calories. The soup was like dishwater. It didn't even contain cheap, rotten turnips. The soup looked like dirt, but because it was hot, we drank it. They also gave each of us a piece of bread. The piece of bread must have been about two inches thick.

I had a choice about what to do with the bread. I could eat it right away and avoid the risk of being robbed, or I could cut it into small, thin pieces to save for later. But I had learned early on that it wasn't safe to keep possessions hidden. Once, in the middle of the night, a man in our group had his throat cut by someone with a knife. The thief slashed him because he wanted to steal his ticket for extra soup the next day. For this reason, whenever I got the soup and the little bread, I ate it up completely, right away.

But something miraculous happened there, even in Buchenwald. I immediately started looking for my brother, because I knew he had been in Buna when we were separated. The day after I arrived in Buchenwald, I ran into the nearest barracks, where the inmates were staring out of the slats like wild dogs. I started yelling, "Gisser, Gisser!" There were many of us looking for our relatives.

I recognized one man who was staring out of the slats; he happened to have been with us in a previous camp. His name was Yankel Gebrovitch. From Radom, he was slightly related to my family. As soon as he heard me call out, "Gisser!" he turned his head around, and yelled to my brother who by some miraculous coincidence was lying there too. "Your brother is here," Gebrovitch announced.

Among 120,000 inmates, I met him in the first barracks! On the second day that I was there! Then we were together. But there was chaos everywhere. There we were together, but it was not for long. They soon organized a transport and my brother was taken to another camp. What could I do? By then we were used to being separated.

# *Among the Dead in Buchenwald*

He went away, and I stayed behind in Buchenwald. The conditions were impossible. We never slept on anything but the wooden boards. And it was very hard. We didn't have water to wash with or to drink. We couldn't wash our faces. The conditions were impossible. There was a toilet which was like a board upon a hole in the ground, and many fell in. It was unbelievable. Every single day there were piles of bodies lined up in front of the buildings, the same way that piles of wood used to be left lying in front of the bakeries in Europe. It was a very grim situation. I was already so weak, so close to dying. Yet we knew that the war was coming to an end. Every day we received news that the German cities were being bombed by the Allies. These reports gave us a hint of hope, though our personal situations still remained grim.

The city next to Buchenwald was Weimar. This city had been pounded badly by the bombing. The Germans needed inmates to dig out the large holes in the ground where the dead were lying. We were the ones who were sent to perform this gruesome task. Quite a scene greeted us when we arrived in Weimar after a night's bombardment. They needed inmates to dig, to find dead people, and it was quite a scene when we would arrive. How well, how respectfully the Germans treated their own dead!

Actually, everyone wanted to get in line to be taken to Weimar for this job, because we thought we would find something to eat in the cellars of the homes in which we were digging. The Germans had stored their confections and jams and potatoes in their bombed-out houses. So we lined up for this kind of work, even though it meant digging up and uncovering dead bodies. At three o'clock in the morning, we had to get in line. This was in March, when it was still quite cold.

I lined up with the others, hoping to be chosen. I didn't look very appetizing because I had on a pair of ragged pants, one leg of which was short and torn, the other very long. And my shoes were torn too. It was cold, but somehow I had acquired a coat. I don't remember where I got it, but I took it with me to be a little warmer. To hold this torn coat together, I took some rope from a clothesline and made a belt to tie the coat across my body to give me a little more warmth. At three o'clock in the morning we stood waiting, and at five o'clock they took us to the train, a regular train, to get to Weimar. It wasn't far; it was only about seven, eight miles down the track.

When we arrived, people were assigned to various areas for digging. What a gruesome mission we had. We were supposed to look for dead people, but we ignored our orders while pretending to obey. Instead, we looked for potatoes, for cellars with potatoes. It was an inclement day, drizzling and wet. We stood there, digging, and digging. We tried to ignore the young *Hitler Jugend* (Hitler Youth) punks who watched us, making fun of us and spitting on us, yelling all kinds of insults. But we remained there for a whole day, and didn't find any food. A Czech foreman was in charge of seeing that we did our work.

I came up in the evening from this mass grave. The foreman noticed that I looked very bad; that I was really close to dying. He had a piece of chewing tobacco; I didn't know what it was, because it looked like a piece of gum, and he gave it to me, probably out of sympathy. I was so starved that I started eating it. I swallowed it because I was so hungry. And right away I felt that I had done something wrong. I felt as if I was really were going to die, so I went over to the foreman, and asked him angrily what he had done to me.

"What did you give me?" I pleaded.

He looked at me, taunting. "I gave you tobacco to chew."

I glared at him in pain, and moaned, "Oh no, I *ate* it."

To this he replied, "You're a stupid ass; that's what you are. Why did you eat this? This is *tobacco*. It's poison to eat it."

He gave me water, as much as I could drink, and then we went to the train to take us back to Buchenwald. I was feeling worse and worse by the minute.

At Buchenwald, another transport had arrived from somewhere, and there was a shortage of bunks for sleeping. It was already dark, after nine o'clock. And I was starving as usual, and I hadn't eaten anything the whole day. I couldn't find my usual sleeping spot, because the bunks had been rearranged for the newcomers. All the bunks had been changed around. These were not even real beds. They were like drawers piled up on top of each other.

I was so exhausted, nauseated, and sick that I wasn't even hungry anymore. I was terribly exhausted, too sick and tired to be hungry anymore. All I wanted was to lay my head down somewhere, so I wandered around, anywhere in the dark, trying to find a place in the absolute darkness. I lay down again and again. And each place I tried to rest was crowded with nervous people also trying to sleep. They would kick me down with their feet, and I was forced to move again and again. I had no place anywhere.

I crawled to yet another place, and the same thing happened. I went to yet another bed, five or six times, upstairs, downstairs, but there were no empty bunks. Finally, I settled into one bunk with a group of quieter people. I lay down, and they didn't kick me. They didn't say anything. It was too quiet. But then I detected a stench and felt it, smelt it. I was lying with dead people. They had put them there.

I threw myself frantically off the high bunk. I fell down, sat up straight, and knelt down in a corner, a pitch-dark enclave, and I started to weep most bitterly, I reminded myself that this was Purim night, the night in March when we would sit and read the Megillah, the Book of Esther. The feeling that came over me was like the feeling I had experienced that faraway Yom Kippur Eve, in the previous camp, after my brother and I had volunteered. All I could think about were the joyous Purims I had spent with my family in Lodz. I could not stop crying. I wept bitterly, and I cursed myself, and I cursed everybody else, and I pleaded.

"Why?" I moaned. "Why do we deserve this?" I didn't say "I" because *I* wasn't alone. "Why do we deserve this miserable lot?" I wept on and on, sitting up for most of the night. I probably fell asleep sitting in this misery. But the next day was a new day, and once more I said, "I'm going to Weimar again."

It was three o'clock in the morning. I was determined to leave the camp once again to dig up the dead. "I am going again," I said, and again I went and again we came to the graves of the people who had been bombed to death in Weimar. The same going, the same digging.

But this time we were luckier. We found potatoes. And the foreman—he was an inmate too—said to us, "Let's get organized. One of you will be on the lookout, and you will let us know if anyone is coming to interrupt us." We took the potatoes and boiled them. They filled a full pail. We called them *Pelkartoffeln,* which means "with the peel, the skin." The potatoes were still dirty, but we didn't care about that. All we wanted was to bite into them. However, I ate so many potatoes right then, that after I was done I prayed, and I wished that I would never have to eat again. All I wanted to do right then was to die. That's how miserable I felt after eating too much. I couldn't bend down anymore. My stomach hurt and it was bloated. My eyes had eaten; my stomach could not. What a misfortune.

This day, like several others, will never be erased from my mind. I still see it before my eyes. What an irony: we found potatoes and we ate them. And I wanted only to die.

# *Ordruff*

In the weeks that followed, we wandered around, aimlessly. There was no work to do. We wandered around and waited for something to happen. One day, after suffering endlessly at this camp, I said to myself, "Why didn't I go with my brother's transport? Why didn't I go away to where my brother went? Why did they leave me out?" So I went into the *Schreibstube,* which was the office for the camp.

A Polish man was sitting there; he was the bookkeeper. I gave him my name, and inquired with some urgency, "Why haven't I been selected to go away from here?" He looked at me and at my name; and again he looked at me and again at my name. I asked, "Is there something wrong? You are looking at me, and at my name."

He replied, "According to our records, you are supposed to be a minor; you are twelve years old! That's the reason that they didn't take you."

They had made a mistake. They had me down as twelve years old. I was glad that I had asked, because on the next day they had another transport. This time, they included me. Again I was with the wagons and the usual transportation; not first class! Eventually we came to a camp that was called Ordruff. When we arrived there, we found other people who told us that this was the place where they manufactured the V1 and the V2 missiles. What were we to do there? We were told that we were going to be put to work.

That night, I was sent to a barracks with seven hundred Russians. It was a huge room, a big barracks. But at first, we had nothing to do. We just sat there, just existing there, not knowing what we were waiting for. Finally a Russian man came over and he was an intelligent man. When he saw me, he advised me right away, saying, "If you don't want to go to work tomorrow morning barefoot, take your shoes and put them around your neck. If you don't do this, you will be walking barefoot in the snow. Here they steal like mad; you don't know what thieves these Russians are. Terrific thieves. Terrific. And their language…"

And this man was a Russian too! I listened to his advice and fastened my shoes together carefully around my neck. These were wooden shoes. One side was worn out and the other was two inches thick. They were extremely uncomfortable. Wood wears out quickly. Sure enough, in the middle of the night I woke up, and somebody was trying to steal my shoes. I woke up and screamed and the thief ran away.

The next morning they loaded us again into the little wagons. They transported stone, dirt, and building material for roads in these vehicles. We were squashed together so tightly. But the tightness actually saved us from falling off and getting trampled. When we arrived at our destination, I was given a shovel and was told to start digging. I looked up and my eyes met those of somebody who stood on the other side. The other man looked at me and said, "Do you know who is here? Your brother is here too."

It was indeed true. My brother was in this camp, and the other worker told me where to look for him. When we came to the barracks later in the day, I went to see him. You can imagine the greeting. I told my brother, "I don't want to stay in my barracks because they will kill me. There are seven hundred Russians there, and everybody is hungry, everybody is nervous, even if there are a few good ones there too."

My brother, by contrast, was in a barracks that was very small. This was because he had arrived earlier. Accordingly, he said to me, "I have an idea."

His idea involved music. Every night there was an orchestra, with the best musicians around, playing for the enjoyment of the Germans. The musicians were from all over, and they really were excellent. My brother suggested, "Maybe you can sing something and they will accompany you. I'll go to my superior and I'll tell him that I want you to be in the same bunk as me."

And lo and behold, we went to the place where the orchestra played, and I went over to the conductor. I begged him, saying, "I need to be able to sing something here. My life depends upon it. I am a singer and my voice is naturally not as good as it was, but I will try my best. Do you have something that I could do?"

The conductor replied, "What can you sing? It has to be in German."

I said, "I'll sing *Dein ist mein ganzes Herz,*" by Franz Lehar, which I happened to know.

To this he replied, "Okay. Let's try it. Let them play a few other pieces and then I will announce that a newcomer is going to perform."

A little while later, I started to sing the German song; I knew the words by heart since I used to sing it before. I received wonderful applause. And right away my brother went over to the man and said, "Can't you do something for him?"

The man replied, "I'll talk to you soon."

That same night I was allowed to get away from the Russian barracks. I was transferred to the new area and was very happy because right then, even though it was four o'clock in the morning, they gave us a little soup. The taste of it was so sharp that it was unbelievable, almost inedible. We ate it, however, because we were so hungry, even though it was so spicy. We ate it because we had no choice, and we also were given a piece of bread. And that night again we had another piece of bread. I told my brother, "This is a wonderful hotel."

In reality, this was actually the worst camp, the one to be dreaded the most. It was here that they planned to finish us off altogether. In this camp—Ordruff—they hoped to kill all of us. Even though they lacked crematoriums, they planned to get rid of us so that we wouldn't be able to tell the Allies what had happened. The English troops were soon expected to arrive.

# *Back to Buchenwald*

When the English indeed came close, the Nazis drove us again back to Buchenwald. We weren't led through the regular roads, which were for the army to pull their equipment, but we walked through the woods. We started walking at night, and it was a dangerous route. Many of us tried to run deeper into the woods, and a lot of inmates were shot. Many actually succeeded in getting away, but it isn't clear that these escapees actually survived their ordeal. Too many of them ended up at the mercy of Germans who were not so kind. Many of them were handed right back to the Nazis.

I too was a victim of sadistic brutality on this harrowing "excursion." I was limping alongside my brother as we marched. We were in a column, and we were being watched over by a cruel guard. I slowly inched my way along, but I had intense pains in my leg and groin. I could barely walk. With each step I took, I felt like I was going to die. The guard took one look at me and said in a menacing voice: "Let me shoot you. I can see that you can't walk." He wanted to do me a favour.

I whispered to my brother, suggesting that we sneak into another column when the guard wasn't looking in our direction. Somehow we managed to move into the column that was marching ahead of us and lost the guard.

And then something else happened. The guards themselves grew tired. One SS guard, weary of wearing a heavy knapsack, gave his possessions to an inmate to hold. How could we resist grabbing his rations? There was food and other supplies in the sack. As soon as it grew dark, we all shared its contents. When the guard realized how he had been duped, he started yelling, "Who did I give it to?" We weren't about to tell him.

We walked until it was about four in the morning. I don't know how I walked; I still don't know how I did it today. I guess I was destined to stay alive. But then something happened. They asked us to lie down because the guards were too tired to walk anymore. So we lay down in a field.

It had been drizzling all through the night, and we were lying down in the wet mud. We lay down but everything was wet and muddy, extremely uncomfortable. I had a thin blanket over me, but it too was muddy and wet. I was dirty, wet, and hungry, hungrier than I had ever been in my life, even at home and throughout my life in the camps. And every few minutes we heard machine guns killing people at will. The Germans saw people and they shot them. The Germans did not stop to ask any questions. And here we were lying, lying in the middle of this madness, afraid to pick up our heads.

Suddenly, there came a relief to my misery. We were with our friend Millstein, who suddenly appeared like an angel from God. He produced a piece of bread that he had saved up, and he shared it with my brother and me. Was this not a gift from heaven? It was only a tiny piece, a minuscule amount of a portion, perhaps just an eighth of a real portion. But it was a piece of sustenance, just a little bit to keep us going. It gave us strength and a little optimism, for not more than an hour later, the Germans roused us again and ordered us to walk. We walked until morning, walking and walking. There were no cars, no vehicles for transports, anymore.

We came back to Buchenwald once more, and it was a different story yet again. This time, they tried to get us away from Buchenwald as soon as possible, as many of us as they could get out of the way. They didn't want too many of us to be around if the Americans should come. They actually wanted to kill us all, but they couldn't. So they concentrated first on getting the Jews off the territory. The SS asked, "Who is a Jew?" and we were ordered once again to march out of the way.

My brother pleaded with me as he had done before. "Maybe we should tear off our special name plates and insignias that show we are Jews. Maybe we should take them off and mix with the other people."

I didn't agree with him. "If we have survived until now as Jews, I want to continue," I responded. "Whatever will happen will happen. Let it happen. I don't want to start pretending now that I am not Jewish. We've made it this far."

# *Workstat*

And so once again there was an announcement that we had to march to somewhere new. They had to take us somewhere, somewhere where we couldn't tell our story. Before we started marching, they stored us in special quarters, in a place called *Workstat*, where they kept nails and wood and building materials. These were special barracks, not the regular ones, where they managed to isolate us. Here there was no luxury of beds or mattresses. There was nothing. It was like a factory. All we could eat were nails or wood. They imposed starvation on us again and again. They didn't want to give us anything. They just wanted us to die.

In the storage barracks we were kept like animals. They locked us in from the outside, and the only way we could see out was through holes in the wood. It seemed as if to torture us further, we could look out to see that they were bringing kettles of soup across the ground. We ached to have that soup, to have anything edible at all, but we didn't know how to get out of the shack. Then suddenly, with all of our strength, we broke the doors. And then we went wild, really wild. Everybody with his little bowl and spoon crashed his way to the soup kettles. As soon as they put the kettles down, we ran over as if in a stampede. The kettles fell down in the dirt.

Our hunger did not bring out sympathy in the SS guards. The high-ranking SS Führer stood mocking us. He looked at us and laughed, saying, "Look at those animals." We had to scrub the liquid from the dirt to drink the soup. The scene was unbelievable. Everyone was wild, scrounging for the merest drop of soup. But to our great disappointment, nobody really retrieved anything, for the liquid had spread all over the ground. It was humiliating to watch the high-ranking, so-called German, the VIP from all the nations, standing up there and laughing at us poor souls.

And this was not the end. Once again, as part of their macabre routine, they announced that they were going to take us out of the camp yet one more time. I was with my brother when they marched us to the gate. We were among the last ones to leave. They said anybody who would march out and not make any trouble would be given a piece of bread to take along. And the people were so hungry and so desperate that they said, "Let's go."

But my brother and I didn't want to march anymore, even though my brother had found a stick that would assist me in walking better. Each time we reached the gate to leave, we changed our minds and walked along to the back of the line again. We didn't want to leave. Indeed, I knew that if we left the camp, we would not survive much longer.

Then, to our good fortune, an alarm suddenly sounded. The sirens signalled a bomb, and we were forced to hide and disperse. The SS ran and dispersed as well, and we were able to run back to a place where young children were lying, too weak and innocent to get away by themselves. They were lying at the front of a barracks. We knew that these were the children whom the Germans didn't want to get rid of.

I don't exactly know what the Germans had planned to do with these children. But we thought it was a good idea to lie down with them, because we knew that they were not going to be sent out of the camp. Perhaps the Germans planned to use them as hostages when the enemy troops arrived.

We lay down there, hoping we were safely hidden. But this was not to be. Soon, the Germans came over to search the area. They wanted to see if other people, like us, were hidden among those poor children. The children were cold and hungry, and many of them had covered themselves with their blankets. We did the same, hoping that we'd be mistaken for teenagers or even younger children. When the guards arrived, they pulled off people's blankets, sorting out the minors from the adults. They found a few people who, like us, were hiding, and naturally they took them out again into the cold night. We could hear the sound of their brutal beatings.

Miraculously, they didn't uncover us or suspect that we were hiding. We remained there, and when the inspection time passed and a big group went out of the camp, the guards gave the order, the command, for everyone to return to the barracks.

We went into one of the barracks, along with countless others. At that time we were mixed with non-Jews: adults, youngsters, everyone mixed together. We didn't know what we were waiting for. To eat: there was nothing distributed to eat. But one man somehow found packages of honey, not liquid, but solid honey in packages, in blocks. He found a few boxes of these and he brought them to us in the barracks. And there was margarine as well. But imagine when you are so hungry, and you haven't eaten in so many days, when you start eating honey and margarine. Imagine how your stomach reacts to this.

Eating proved to be a disaster for me. I became so sick that I lay down nauseous near the door, with a high fever. My brother couldn't do anything for me, and I had no idea of how to treat my symptoms. I actually lay there for a few days.

# *Liberation*

Finally, it was the eleventh of April, three o'clock in the afternoon. The Allied troops arrived to rescue us. The camp was in total chaos. Many of the German guards had already run away themselves, out of fear of being taken captive. The inmates themselves were watching at the guard posts. All of a sudden, one fearful man jumped away from the window—he was sitting on a window ledge—and in a frightened voice announced, "Oh, they are finally going to finish us off!" But the troops that were arriving were not German. A Russian inmate jumped to the window and yelled, "*Duren*—idiot—this is an *American* tank!"

And so it was at three o'clock in the afternoon, on the eleventh of April, when the first American tank came in. We were finally to be liberated. Some of the guards met a deserved, crueler fate, as they were taken down from their posts by the inmates, and were beaten to smithereens. These guards were the stupid ones who had stayed behind; the SS had had enough foresight to have gone away already. Many guards were caught later on; we brought them back to the camp; they were not only beaten up but were so beaten up that they were full of blood. Nonetheless, they didn't die—enough of them are probably in Canada today. They didn't die, because the Americans were not as cruel as the Germans, supposedly the most intelligent nation in the world.

This was the first day of our liberation.

After we were liberated, we stayed in the SS barracks for a few days. However, the friendly troops eventually located us in the barracks where the SS had been. The Nazi guards naturally had run away, so we took over. And the troops created a hospital for those of us who had become sick. There were doctors looking after us, and the imprisoned German orderlies, as well, were forced to help out in the hospitals.

The Russian survivors became our cooks, and whatever they found that was edible, they put into the kettles. They had such big kettles that ten people could get into them. We were given packages from the SS which those beasts had gotten from home: packages with cookies, chocolate, and other goodies. They put whatever they could find into the kettle, plus potatoes and anything else that was edible. Imagine what this kind of diet did for the starving people. Imagine what our stomachs were like. Thousands of us died even after our liberation.

I became sick and I didn't know why. I had been sick even before we had been liberated, but now there was enough food to eat. The Americans also brought in all kinds of food that I couldn't eat; that is how sick I felt. I couldn't eat, and my brother grew furious. He said, "Until now, you were starving! And now we have food and you can't eat! *Why* don't you eat?"

I replied, "I just can't eat; I don't *know* what the matter is." And I couldn't walk either.

One day my brother was particularly hungry. But again, I

refused to eat. I said to myself, "I'm going to the hospital now, by myself."

When I got there, the Polish doctor took one look at the way I looked, and he examined me immediately. He then gave me seven pills to ingest right then. I remember them quite clearly. There were four black ones and three white ones, or vice versa, but after I took them, I didn't remember anything.

But my poor brother didn't know where I was. He spent the whole day looking for me. Finally, someone told him that they had seen me entering the hospital. He rushed over to the hospital that evening, and asked for me, calling out my name. The Polish doctor replied, "Yes, he is here, but I don't think he is going to live. He won't make it because he has typhoid and pneumonia. Both."

He had knocked me out with the pills. But miraculously, I woke up when my brother was standing over me. He told me that he had been looking for me, and was angry that I hadn't told him where I was going.

I remained in this hospital for four weeks, and I couldn't even eat the miserable cream of wheat that they kept feeding me. And cream of wheat was one of my favourite foods. It was sweet but I had no appetite for it.

Every day, they brought new sick people into the hospital. I remember one, a Hungarian named Mermelstein. Everybody thought that he was dead. And we wondered, "What is a dead person doing in here?" They brought him in, and we surely believed he was dead, lying on his bed.

One man said, "Why did you bring him here?"

The doctor patted him on his shoulder and said, "We'll fix him up. He will run after the women yet." We thought he was dead but the doctors knew better.

A few days later, Mermelstein stole all the margarine and all the bread that was at the other patients' beds. He stole everything.

I couldn't eat the kind of food that they were doling out to us. So my brother went all the way down to Weimar, the big city, and managed to acquire eggs, onions, and potatoes for me. He came back to camp and cooked my meals for me. He took two bricks and made a little fire between them, behind the window where I was lying. It was in a forested area, and when they caught him, they wanted to kill him. But he managed to run away, and then came back to give me my meals through the window. This was not allowed; patients are never allowed to have their food delivered to the hospital. But what he brought me I was able to eat! And he saved me! Thanks to him, I remained alive.

After four weeks, I was released. I was extremely weak and thin. In the forest surrounding the hospital, there was a little tree with a diameter of less than ten inches, maybe just six inches. But I couldn't lift my foot to go over it; that's how weak I was.

Did we have a destination? Finally they started registering us. We were asked to provide our names, ages, and places of birth. They started to make us little passports. This was done while I was in the hospital. My brother did it for me, signed for me, and I still have my passport to this very day, my Buchenwald passport. He forged my signature and I still have this too.

Then we heard that we could now leave, to go wherever we wanted. "You are free," they announced. They asked us, "Who wants to go back to Poland?"

What reason did we have for returning to Poland? Everyone we knew had been sent to Auschwitz. As for going to Israel, that was a land open only to a group of young, very young people. (When they came there, the English didn't let them in, but that's a different story.)

My brother and I decided that we would get out of the section of the country we were in, because we heard that this area was going to be occupied by the Russians. We started out on our own, with only our backpacks in our possession. We moved as fast as we could, because we didn't want to be under Russian domination. We saw a locomotive, and we asked the German driver, "Where are you going?" He mentioned a place, and we asked, "Are you going any farther to the West?"

He said, "*Jawohl,* yes, certainly." So we sat up in the coal department of the train, and we were traveling, and going and going and going. When it grew a little dark outside, the driver stopped so that we could get off the train. Soon we found a little town where there was a *Burgermeister,* a mayor. When we showed the people our little passports, they gave us stamps for food, and gave us some money and also lodging to stay overnight. I don't even remember the name of this town, but it was on the road to get away from Germany.

They assigned us to a family overnight. This was the first night, after so many years, that we slept in a real bed, with white linen, and real sheets. We were given a wonderful, beautiful supper. The house belonged to two elderly women— I don't know where the men were—two sisters. When we told them where we came from, they started to cry. And they really treated us wonderfully.

In the morning we again went out and tried to find a way to continue traveling. We wanted to go to the big camp called Bergen Belsen. This camp was being supervised by English troops now; the English occupied this camp. We hoped to find some other people who were like us, because we were alone. So we found a train that was going in the right direction. It was bitter cold, and we traveled all through the night. The next day, before eating, we finally made our way to Bergen Belsen.

In Bergen Belsen, we recognized a few people whom we had known in our camp. We even met friends whom we had known in Poland. And I also met a young girl. She has grandchildren now, but at that time she was just fifteen years old, and she wanted to get out of Bergen Belsen. Naturally she had no parents; she was completely alone. And she was very beautiful too. Seven of us then banded together, and we said that we were going to travel back into Germany, toward Frankfurt, to one of the larger centres where Jews might be. Perhaps we could find some civilization there. The young girl said that she really wanted to go with us, but that she was afraid. I was just about the oldest in the group, and I wanted to reassure her. "I will take you with me, wherever I end up," I said. "You won't ever have to worry."

We came to a little bit of a town, and again, we followed the same routine. They found us a hotel. The other boys wanted to have a good time; naturally, for five years they hadn't been with a girl. They went, and I stayed with this fifteen-year-old girl, and I kept my word. I protected her all the way.

The name of this little town was Dilenburg. It wasn't far from Frankfurt-am-Main. In this town, we met a chaplain by the name of Herschel Schechter. He was the one who had been present at the liberation of Buchenwald, and he conducted services on Friday nights with the Jewish GIs. For the first time, I heard melodies that were the customary prayers in the United States. Chaplain Schechter asked us, "Where are you going? Where do you want to go?"

We answered, "We don't know where to go. We are just wandering around. We are thinking of going to Frankfurt-am-Main."

He responded, "Why don't you go to a little town called Wetzlar?"

Wetzlar is a small historic town where Leica cameras are produced. The owner of the Leica factory was named Leitz, and he lived in a special castle. His was a family of great distinction. We asked Schechter, "Why should we go to Wetzlar?"

To which he replied, "There is a man in the army who is the head of the CIC (like the FBI). He happens to be a very religious man. He is from the Frankfurt ultra-Orthodox community. And he will take care of you. Once you meet him, they will do everything possible to help you establish yourselves. He will help you out for the time being."

We did exactly what he asked.

We came to Wetzlar, and we met this man named Neuberger. When he heard that we were coming, and what we had been through, naturally he became very sentimental and very helpful to us. The first thing he did was to find us a place to live. He took a country club area that belonged to an organization, Jacht House. He took it away from the Germans and gave it to us. We were given rations of food and anything else we needed. We didn't do anything there, but we tried to keep ourselves occupied. Everybody went their own way. Somebody wanted to start a little business in dealing with the black market, buying diamonds with coffee. The Germans were dying for coffee.

# My Surviving Brothers

My brother loved to wander around, to go, to see, to meet people. One day, I saw him coming down the street, with two boys at his side. And when he came closer, *I recognized my other two brothers.* They happened to have arrived unexpectedly. We never dreamt that anyone else from our family was still alive. We had long ago given up hope. But these were my two young brothers who had survived.

They went through hell ten times over in a little camp that belonged to Dachau. It was called Kaufering. I had a third brother there, who unfortunately didn't live in the same barracks. Every day, they visited him, but one day they came to see him and he was gone. He had died, like many, many thousands of others.

We heard the story of how they had come to this little town to see us. There was a man who had some business transactions with other camps. He went to a camp called

Lansburg, near Bayern, near Munich. This man was telling the people about two brothers—*us*—both of whom were cantors and singers. There was a young man sitting there, listening to this story. The man who was listening suddenly jumped up and said, "How is it? We have two brothers too, who are still in the hospital, and they told us that they had a brother who was a cantor, and that they come from a musical family." He asked, "What is the name?" and the man replied, "Gisser." The man said, "I think that this is the same name!"

And lo and behold, he came back and went to this hospital. He ran up and told my two brothers about us, and they couldn't wait to be released. They were quite sick. They had survived under the worst conditions; they could write a book about just one night that they had lived through.

They ran away and found a train that went in our direction. It was so crowded that they had to push themselves in through the window, though people helped them. This is how they came to us, and we couldn't have imagined that something like this could possibly have happened. It was too much of a coincidence.

# Chanting Prayers in Germany

I was with my brother, and I decided that I wanted to study. Somebody told us about a man who was a composer of great distinction. They advised me to look him up. I went with my brother, who was not at that time very much interested in singing. I, however, wanted to study as well as sing.

I met a man named Gustav Adolph Schlemm. He was living in this castle and was related to the daughter of Mr. Leitz. One evening, a great opera singer came to perform. After the concert, he came over. His name was Gonschar, and he was a very wonderful baritone who sang all the leading roles in the Frankfurt Opera. He said he wanted to hear me, and I sang a piece of *Chazzanut*, a liturgical piece. They were all taken with it. My voice was already coming back a little bit, and musically I was very well situated. I knew a little about opera since before the war I had sung *La Traviata* in Yiddish. So I sang all kinds of oratorios and songs, and took to this kind of repertoire very well. Thus, I was somewhat able to establish myself in this little town.

In the meantime, I had made my acquaintance with a Jewish chaplain named Blinder. He was at that time the chaplain for Heidelberg and Mannheim, cities not far from the little town where I lived. He had heard of me, and thought that he might be able to find me a cantorial position. Why? Because Neuberger, the man who took care of us, wanted to revive and rebuild a little synagogue that was in this town. It was a very beautiful, picturesque synagogue that had not been completely destroyed. He decided that with funds from the German government, he could hire me as the cantor for the time being.

We didn't have much luck with this, because there were only seven Jews in the group, and maybe another two or three who were half Jewish. We tried to hold our services. The synagogue had just been rebuilt, and we could have our services there.

One day, however, Chaplain Blinder said that I might have more success in the city of Mannheim. There I could find a Jewish center, with a synagogue that desperately needed a cantor.

"We want you to come for a dedication, to dedicate the new synagogue there," he told me. Even so, it wasn't really a synagogue; it was more like a hall. But when I went there I performed a religious service with this chaplain, and they were really taken with me because by then my voice was again very good. We dedicated the synagogue. There was a general in charge at that time; he was a member of the Jewish welfare board and he ordered me, *really* ordered me, saying, "You have to take this job in Mannheim. There's work to do in Heidelberg as well. They are two cities that don't have a cantor. We need services for our people."

I took the job, and although the chaplain was a very religious man, we performed the services on Friday night in one city, and the next morning took a jeep and drove to Heidelberg to hold the services there. Sometimes we reversed the order of cities on Friday night and Saturday morning. They paid me a salary too; and the salary was enough to buy two cartons of cigarettes on the black market. But this wasn't important. We already were receiving our rations from the UNRWA (United Nations Relief and Works Agency).

I lived in Mannheim on the weekends. One day I received a phone call from my brother who was still is Wetzlar. He said, with some mystery in his voice, "I have met two young girls. They want to join our group. One is very pretty. I wish you could come home. Maybe you could marry one of them."

One wasn't so pretty; the other was very pretty. To make the story short, I came home and I liked her very much. Her name was Anna.

# *Anna*

My wife Anna, of blessed memory, was born in July 1925. She came from a very distinguished family in Krakow. She had a sister and a brother and she alone survived the war. When Anna had just turned fifteen, the war broke out, and her family was sent into the Krakow ghetto. This was the worst ghetto of all. Anticipating that the family would not survive, Anna's parents decided to send her away to live with a Gentile family.

To Anna's horror, informers reported that there was a Jewish girl living among the Poles. She was immediately called to the Gestapo, who set about torturing her. They persisted in asking her about her origins, but she wouldn't admit anything. She was instead stubbornly insistent, repeatedly saying, "I am not Jewish." Finally, they stopped interrogating her, but then they sent her to a camp, where she was mixed into a group composed of many different nationalities.

When I met her she was in a camp called Braunschweig, near Hanover, and the camp had already been liberated. Right after the liberation she was wandering around other camps with her good friend. Both of them were trying to get established somewhere; they were also searching for people they knew who might have survived. One day they heard that there was a big camp in Wetzlar, where my brother and I had been, so they decided to settle there and at least be among Jews.

My brother met the two girls just by coincidence. One day they started talking. Even though my brother wasn't married, he wanted me to meet these girls first. He thought that one of them might interest me.

"You've got to meet these two very nice women," he said. "One of them, Anna, is especially beautiful, though the other one, Hanka, is a fine person too."

Curious, I drove the eighty miles by car, and I met Anna for the first time. I liked her very much, but I had a problem because I didn't know what to say to her friend Hanka. I couldn't marry both of them!

I tried very hard to get Hanka matched up with another man. The man whom she soon found was about twenty years older than she was, and he acted like a daddy to her. He was a very religious man. But she was glad not to be alone, and I appreciated the opportunity to get to know Anna better without feeling guilty about her friend. We started to see each other seriously around January 1946.

In August 1946 Anna and I got married. It was a civil marriage first, followed by a religious ceremony in September.

# Marriage and Family

My congregation in Mannheim was overjoyed that Anna and I were going to get married. With so much sadness in everybody's life, it was rare for Jews in Europe to celebrate a happy event.

The congregation insisted that we make the wedding there. But to make a wedding was not as easy then as it is today, when you go to a caterer, pay, and the party planners take care of the details. Instead, I had to go to the UNRWA's headquarters in Heidelberg to get cans of food and other provisions for the wedding. Because of my position as cantor, I couldn't just make a small wedding for the congregation.

Then my brother had an idea. He said, "Let's go to a farm in Wetzlar. It's not far. You can buy a lamb and go to Frankfurt to a kosher slaughterer. One lamb ought to provide enough meat for all of your guests."

And that is exactly what we did. We went to a farm, and

the owner took us around, trying to convince us to purchase a certain lamb. He said, "This is the lamb that I want to give you. It's a very good one." My brother and I looked at the poor lamb, who was bleating and staring up at us as if it were pleading with us to save its life. We just couldn't feel right about killing it. We said, finally, "If we are going to have a good time, then it seems wrong and unjust to take the life of this little lamb." We left without the lamb.

We weren't in the best of moods on our wedding day. My parents were dead; most of my family wasn't there; they were all gone. And Anna, my bride, had no one. No one at all. She had survived alone. She didn't have a father or a mother, no sisters, no brothers, no uncles nor aunts. She was completely alone. And this fact only added to my grief, because I felt very bad that she had nobody. At least I had a few remaining brothers. Three brothers and myself.

The chaplain's name was Dicker. He was a very fine man. Unfortunately, during the whole wedding ceremony, under the canopy, both Anna and I were crying and not a person could stop us. She cried because she didn't have anyone. No one in the world. I cried because I didn't have all of us. My parents and the rest of my family were gone.

It was turning into a very tragic event. Finally, in his speech the rabbi suddenly said to me, "I don't understand why you are both so upset. Why do you cry so much? I know you miss your families, but so do others. And knowing you, you are someday going to be a very happy man." And then he turned to my wife, and pleaded, "You are going to be happy too. This is a wedding; stop crying!"

The wedding was fine in the end. The people had a good time, but the next day, unfortunately, I realized that I hardly had money to buy breakfast. I was almost completely penniless.

I had to turn then to a friend who was a witness at the wedding. Today he is retired but he eventually had taken a job as a director of Hillel at Harvard University (he graduated from the Jewish Theological Seminary, a brilliant man by the name of Benzion Gold). At the time, he was employed by the army as a provisions director. So he lent me a few hundred marks so that I could start my life again.

But it was very hard. My financial condition was desperate. My double salary for being a cantor in two places was just enough to buy two pounds of coffee and two cartons of cigarettes on the black market. To supplement these small earnings, I taught, sang, and gave concerts. And somehow Anna and I managed to make it through each month.

# At the Conservatory

At the end of 1946, I was accepted at the conservatory in Heidelberg, the Hochschule für Musik. My dream was to become an opera singer, and finally I began to see this dream materialize.

At the conservatory, I was able to study with the finest teacher. His name was Richard Schubert. They said he had played the greatest Eleazar (a role in *La Juive*) ever; he was a tenor. But unfortunately he was not a consistent tenor; he was really a high baritone who sang tenor because he had a high baritone voice. Sadly, he had lost his voice quite early. He was about fifty-five years old at the time I knew him.

I was his best pupil. He always admired how I had the ability to perform coloraturas. One day, I sang Mozart's *Hallelujah* chorus while the dean of the music school was behind the door, listening to my baritone. This Mozart piece is not easy to sing because of all the coloraturas. Schubert admired it so much that he opened up the door and said, "There is someone I would like you to meet. Here is a pupil who dares to sing *Hallelujah* by Mozart."

Schubert and I became good friends. Later, we collaborated on various works. I studied with him until 1949. Over those years, I got acquainted with many people from the world of opera. One evening, all the directors of the other opera houses in the region came to listen to the new people from our school. I sang that night with a soprano, a beautiful girl with a gorgeous voice. Together we sang the Rigoletto duet, and then I sang an aria from Meyerbeer, *La Africaner*. After that performance, I received an invitation to sing the main role in Wiesbaden. Wiesbaden is not far from Frankfurt.

But I couldn't take this job. I thought about it, but I already had my little girl, who was then about two years old. I said, "Why should I stay here in Germany?" There was no way that I could imagine bringing her up in Germany. And so, I decided not to stay.

# *Helen*

In 1947 Anna and I still lived with the large group of our friends and my brothers in the house in Wetzlar. There were always at least twelve of us: eight or nine young men, and two or three young women. And in 1947 my daughter Helen was born, and she was a premature child.

We believed that Anna was only six months pregnant. She went into labour suddenly, in the middle of a February night. And it was stormy and chilly when I had to run out quickly to find the doctor. A big storm had started the night before, and it was impossible for me to drive my car.

The doctor agonized about what to do. Because the baby was premature, the local hospital would be unequipped to deal with her physical condition. The doctor didn't want to risk taking her there. Unlike me, however, he was able to drive his car, and he rushed Anna away to the larger town of Giessen, about fifteen kilometers away.

We drove through the snow, with great difficulty. At the hospital in Giessen, a young German doctor looked at Anna and said that he refused to proceed with the delivery. Anna had already lost all of her water, and the hospital didn't have the necessary equipment to proceed with this kind of a birth. The doctor wanted instead to send us to a neigbouring little town.

"No way," I said. "There is no way that I will do this; I will not go away from this hospital. I can't go any farther. Even if I will die, I am going to stay here." After we argued for awhile, he saw my predicament and attempted to undertake delivering the baby. I sat in a waiting room, fearing the worst.

But after about an hour, the doctor opened the door to the waiting room and said, "You have a daughter, but she is very, very, very tiny." My heart was filled with thankful emotion, even though the doctor seemed so cautious when he declared that the baby would have to remain in the hospital for at least a month.

And that is exactly what happened. The baby was the smallest child I had ever seen. They didn't have incubators at that time, so they wrapped her in warm cotton. She still had hair on her cheeks. She was very fragile. Five weeks later, we took baby Helen home.

Helen is named after my grandmother, my mother's mother. We could have named her after so many of our murdered relatives, but we chose to call her after my grandmother. I was afraid to name her after one of my parents, because in truth I still wasn't sure that my parents were dead. With that little bit of doubt and hope still remaining, I didn't want to give her a name for someone who might still have been alive. In Hebrew she is Chaya Rasha. *Chaya* usually is associated with life.

Over the five weeks that Helen was in special care, we searched unsuccessfully to find a nurse for her. We knew that we needed help with such a small child. But the German nurses were afraid of us. They knew how suspicious we were of the Germans, and they feared that if something bad were to happen to the infant, we would blame them and say that they did it purposely. Each time I found a potential nurse, she would say apologetically, "I'm sorry. I can't take care of this child. I'm very sorry." Finally we found a woman who agreed to care for Helen, but she would only work in her own home. She said, "Bring the baby here. I will nurse her here." We were grateful that our search had ended.

But one day, our neighbour came running over to us, advising us to take our baby home as soon as possible. "Do you know what she does to your baby?" our neighbour said. "She puts the crib out on the roof, near the chimney, and leaves her there all day. How can you give away your child to this person who calls herself a nurse? Your baby spends the whole day crying next to the chimney." What an awful image after Auschwitz.

Immediately I brought Helen back to our house. Anna and I had to take care of her alone. We were still so inexperienced ourselves; certainly we had no knowledge about raising a weak baby. Anna was younger than me, and we missed having our own parents to assist us. I undertook to do many of the chores. I gave her a bath, and I fed her with tiny bottles. I did a very good job! Later on, we found someone else who was able to help out. But it wasn't easy; it was a very trying time.

In addition, Helen developed asthma. We nursed her once in the middle of the night, and finally had to go to the hospital because she couldn't breathe. There they gave her a turpentine bath, which was not too appetizing.

Helen was fortunate, in one way, to live in a very active house where she received a lot of love and attention. She couldn't have known about our lonely loss of family, for at that time we lived with my brothers, all sharing a house. My brother Hyman in particular had tremendous patience, and he helped a great deal with my daughter's growing up. He took her out for walks, played with her, and went with her to the park.

I tried to work and to help rebuild the Jewish community. There was a lot to do. I remember, for example, that I had an exciting invitation to sing in Wetzlar, at a new camp for Jews who had come from Russia. There were five thousand people in the camp, and they needed to build a *mikvah* (a ritual bath). There was a very orthodox rabbi there, a scholarly *Rov* (a dintinguished rabbi). He asked me to give a concert, without remuneration, and whatever money the performance generated would be donated to build the mikvah.

I immediately agreed. It was in the winter. The concert hall was really a huge barracks that could seat a thousand people. I came wearing tails, for I thought that a concert hall merited this type of dress. I borrowed the tails and I came and sang a complete concert alone. Later, I received a beautiful letter from the Rov; I still have it. He praised me to the sky and was grateful. They made 5,000 marks to build the mikvah, and I got the credit for it.

I also gave concerts in other camps. My impresario made sure that I had a soprano to accompany me. She was not Jewish but she sang Yiddish beautifully. She also sang Hebrew liturgical pieces, and we always received a standing ovation. I recall giving concerts in Landsberg, Feldafing, Munich, Frankfurt, Stuttgart, and many other places.

I wasn't earning a lot of money, but I gained increasing prestige.

# *Amsterdam*

I had made the decision not to stay in Germany, when I saw an advertisement in the newspaper for a position in Amsterdam. The liberal synagogue—liberal, not meaning Reform, but a traditional service that nonetheless used an organ on *Shabbat* (the Sabbath)—was looking for a cantor. I immediately replied to the advertisement, stating that if they were interested, I would come for an audition. To my astonishment, a man called up quite soon after, saying that he was from Amsterdam and that he wanted to come over right then to talk to me. He said he had gotten a call from the synagogue. He was a wholesale dealer in watches, and he often had business in Germany. He came up to the house. We greeted each other pleasantly. But he was apologetic.

"I don't know anything about singing, about voices," he explained. So I said that I would sing something for him so that he could at least hear my voice. But he replied, "I am not a *maven*, a connoisseur. I won't know anything about it. But the way you are talking, where you studied, what you did, I take your word about your qualifications. I'm impressed with you. You will hear from us about coming here for the high holidays."

They only needed someone for the high holidays in Amsterdam. And soon enough, I received their letter confirming my appointment, and I packed my things. Because of the visa situation, I could only go by myself; I had to leave my wife and child behind because the work request was only for me.

When I arrived at the train station in Amsterdam, the whole executive board was there to greet me. I had a lot of books and heavy suitcases, but everybody gave me a hand. Most of the congregants in Amsterdam were German Jews. Among the people who greeted me that day was Anne Frank's father, Otto Frank. He was to become my best friend in that city. He would come every Friday night to have dinner with us.

Otto Frank was an extremely fine man. On my first day in Amsterdam, he picked me up in the morning, and the first thing he did was to show me the place where he had been hidden with his family. Otto also introduced me to something else that I have never forgotten. In Amsterdam at that time, husbands and wives would stand together in a little booth, selling herrings. The man would prepare the herrings, and the wife would chop the onions. This was such a delicacy that I couldn't stop eating. I must have eaten three herrings the first time I walked around with Otto Frank. He was amazed at my appetite.

After a few days, I met the organist of the synagogue, a man named Mr. Duche. He was an elderly gentleman who had previously been an organist in Aachen, at one of the biggest churches. He was my accompanist. Together, we prepared to rehearse.

I came up, ready to sing, only to shock myself by discovering that suddenly I had no voice whatsoever! I couldn't figure out why. I didn't have a cold, but I still found it impossible to sing. I grew frantic, but the organist was comforting to me.

He said, "Don't feel bad; I know why this has happened. Sometimes when you arrive in a place that has a different climate, this can happen."

They gave me the address of a doctor, a wonderful woman who looked in my throat and said, "Your vocal cords are as red as fire. You have an infection and you have to be on medication. You won't be able to sing for a few days."

And that is exactly what happened. In a few days, I was ready to sing again. The organist gave me a book by Levandosky, a German composer who had written liturgical works for choirs. It was a huge book to study, and I started reading it from start to finish.

The high holidays services were different in Holland than they are in North America. In North America, the main cantor takes the major parts, and the assistant cantor also sings a number of important pieces. In Amsterdam, however, only one cantor leads the entire service. So I started from the very beginning, and the organist accompanied me. He was quite surprised that I was able to follow the music so quickly. He asked me if I had ever sung some of the songs, and I relied, "No. Certain numbers I have, but not everything."

He replied, "But you aren't stopping at all. We are going through this as if it were an actual performance."

"What did you expect?" I replied. "I am reading it from sight, like I am reading a book."

And in two hours, we had almost finished the whole service. He called up the board and said, "I have never seen anything like this. In addition to having a beautiful voice, this cantor can read like no one else I have ever seen."

For the holy days, they rented a large concert hall. About nine hundred people attended services on the first night of Rosh Hashanah, the Jewish New Year. The high holidays went so well, that when they were over, I received a beautiful letter from the congregation. The letter said that the synagogue unfortunately couldn't keep their word to let me go home. Instead, they asked me to remain in Amsterdam for at least two years. They would not take no for an answer. Thus for two years I worked on Friday nights. During the week I was free to do whatever I wanted.

After two years, I decided that I wanted to move on. I had given concerts in Amsterdam, big concerts with distinguished choirs, and I also had sung on the radio. But I was not earning enough to live on. When it came time to negotiate my salary for the year 1951, I asked the synagogue to include a special additional salary just for the high holidays. But they were very insulted that I wanted special money for the holidays. They replied by writing me a letter saying that I was free to leave. My wife started to cry, because with what I had been earning, I hadn't been able to save a penny. I was like a fish out of water. I said, "Don't cry," and went over to the phone and called a congregation in Rotterdam. It was a very, very religious congregation, but I knew that even though I was in a liberal synagogue, they would accept me because they knew that inwardly I wasn't a liberal cantor. They knew that I came from a Hasidic family.

I called up and they said, "Come right down." They didn't have a cantor for the holidays, and I knew it. "Come right down."

By the time I got there, about two hours later by train, there were fifteen people including the rabbi sitting and waiting for me. I came in and introduced myself. They asked me, "What would you like?"

To which I replied, "Two thousand gulden."

My previous salary for a whole month had been just 375 gulden. They said, "If you don't mind, we would appreciate it if you would leave us for a few moments so that we can have a discussion."

I went out of the room, and it didn't take a minute until they called me back in. They opened the door and said, "Come in. The job is yours. You'll get what you want." They told me what their requirements were. And I know that I did a magnificent job for the holidays. After Simchat Torah (the fall holy day celebrating the conclusion and the beginning of the annual cycle of reading the Torah), I performed one more time in Amsterdam.

Anna and I were determined, however, to leave Europe. Right after these events, we decided to sell our apartment and furniture. I found a buyer right away and we went to stay in a hotel. The next morning, we were on our way back to Mannheim, where my brothers were still living. They had a little business but it wasn't thriving. Fortunately they didn't go bankrupt when we all decided to leave. They just left, closing the doors and walking out.

We were really penniless when we decided to leave for Canada.

# Going to Canada

Like so many other immigrants, we had to deal with numerous levels of bureaucracy before we could travel to Canada. Before we got our visas, we had to deal with the red tape of the Canadian consulate in Germany.

I told the consul that I was a carpenter. Canada at that time needed carpenters and shoemakers, but not cantors. I had a certificate from someone in Mannheim, saying that I was qualified to do carpentry wherever I would go. But when the consul took one look at me, he immediately asked, "Could I see your hands?" I showed him my hands. "Some carpenter you are," he said. There was scorn in his voice. I started to reply but it was now lunch time. The consul looked at his watch and said, "Okay. I'm sorry. We will have to see you afterwards."

As I sat in the reception area, I noticed that nine out of ten Jewish people's applications for visas were rejected. They came out of their interviews and were rejected, rejected. This only seemed to happen to the Jews; all the other nationalities came out with smiles on their faces. They were all accepted.

I decided to appeal to the consul. Before he left the building for lunch, I said to him firmly, "We are here, six people. My brothers, my wife, and my child. If even one of us is rejected, nobody will be able to go because we are a close family. If you reject one, you will reject all of us." I spoke to him in not-bad English. It was clear that he understood me. And later that day, he gave us permission to leave for Canada.

The actual trip to Canada was another harrowing experience. I was sick with pneumonia for two weeks before we were supposed to leave. I needed to have injections every day. It was very, very tragic. We thought for sure that I wouldn't make it. My whole family prayed that I would be allowed to board the ship when we went to Bremen, where we would catch the ship to Halifax.

Somehow, I was well enough. I made it. When we boarded the ship, we realized that there were three thousand people on the ship, very few of whom were Jews. Most of the people were SS Germans traveling on false papers, with false names. Many called themselves Altman, because the name could be either a Jewish or a German name. They came en masse. Unfortunately, we went through hell again until we arrived in Canada.

Our voyage was very stormy. It was the cold Christmas season, and we spent twelve days on the ocean. For several days we went through a terrible, terrible storm, and the boat was small and crowded, again with nearly three thousand people upon it. Eating at a table was impossible. Most of the people were lying in bed, nauseous and shaking with the wind for most of the trip. The storm was so bad that after we arrived, the captain told us that we had been in great danger.

In Halifax, we were each given five dollars, since we were penniless. I will never forget that the first thing we tasted in

Canada was apples. We had never eaten such beautiful apples.

Anna, Helen, and I were sent to lodge with a family in Montreal. Their name was Kogen, and they lived in a little duplex in Outremont. We arrived in the evening and the lady of the house—her husband was working—asked me, "What do you do for a living?" I said, "I am a singer."

She said, "Ugh, terrible. It's no good. If only you were a cantor instead."

I replied somewhat reluctantly, "You know, I *am* a cantor too."

The reason I had said that I was a singer was because I didn't want to be a cantor any longer, in the worst way. I really wanted to be an opera singer, but how could I achieve this dream when I didn't have even a penny? The Metropolitan Opera wasn't exactly waiting for me! So I said, "If you want, then I am a cantor too."

Things immediately began to fall into place. Indeed, something very funny happened. Mrs. Kogen said, "My husband's boss"—her husband was a butcher—"is making a bar mitzvah and it's in a small synagogue not far from here. Maybe if you say that you are a cantor, he will invite you too. And if you can sing something and someone hears you, then maybe you can get a position here in Montreal. Once you have a position as a cantor you will be able to make some money."

I said, "Fine," and I was really happy.

When her husband came home from work, she told him what she had told me. He said, "Sure. I will get him an invitation. Let's see what happens."

And what happened was exactly what they had predicted. I sang one number, because they told me to sing just one piece. But after this one piece, they asked me to continue singing. And there was a couple there by the name of Mr. and Mrs. Speirs, who belonged to Shaare Zion Congregation, where I still sing today. They said, "Did you know that our synagogue is looking for a cantor? They have almost hired one, but the contract isn't signed yet. And you sing much better than he does. We're going to call the right people for you. And you will get a call from us tomorrow morning."

And sure enough, the next morning, one of the vice presidents called. He asked me to come over to Shaare Zion. When I started to sing, about ten people were listening to me. But by the time I finished there were fifty people listening. They called around while I was singing. After my audition, they wanted me to perform a service on the next Shabbat. And I have remained at Shaare Zion for over 45 years.

# *David*

Five months after I arrived in Montreal, my son David was born. What a contrast it was to that stormy February night in Germany when Helen came into the world. When he was born, I was a little more established, it was a normal birth, and we were able to celebrate with a party. I was already the cantor at Shaare Zion, and we invited the board of the synagogue to dinner at the time of David's *brith* (circumcision). Cantor Mendelson, of blessed memory, of the Shaar Hashomayim synagogue, was the *moyel* (a person who performs ritual circumcision).

    We named the baby David after my own brother. I knew that he had died because he had entered the concentration camp with my other two brothers. They knew that he had passed away one night. His name had been Zvi David. This time, I knew for certain that I could give my son his name.

    My brother David had been a young man of no nonsense.

He was about six years older than me. A natural intellectual, he had wanted to gain an education and he taught himself. He even knew how to speak English, and spoke German well because he had a German partner in his business.

He had a factory before the war began, but he struggled hard to make a living. Unfortunately, he couldn't afford to hire good workers. I was only about fourteen years old when I started working for him. Once I worked forty hours without stopping! That day, when I was hungry and thought that my family was going to bring something to eat from the house, all they brought me was tomato soup. Tomatoes were very cheap; they gave them away for almost nothing.

My brother owned the factory, but when the Germans came in, he, like other Jews, had to hand his factory over and go to work for them. He was a very sincere person, and he refused to live through this injustice.

Once he cried out to a German in the ghetto, "You don't have a *Gericht,* you don't have a court. You have a *Fistgericht,* a false court. Your court is with a fist and with a gun."

In response, the German said he would inform the authorities about my brother. "Do you know that for this I can report you to the authorities?"

# My Other Brothers

Meyer

My brother Meyer was two and a half years older than me. He was not a great singer, but even like the rest of us he was musical. But he didn't get into it like I did. He was an artist instead. From the time he was ten years old, he would buy himself pencils and charcoal for drawing and sketching. He painted with oils on canvas, and even his early attempts were quite good. He learned all by himself, never taking a lesson from anyone. How sad this was, because he could have been a fine painter. He was working very hard as a cutter of turcots and knits. They didn't have the machines like they do today, so he worked with a big knife, fifteen inches long. He'd cut the whole day. Sometimes in the high season, the factory needed a lot of goods, so they would lock Meyer in from the outside, not even providing him with a telephone.

He would work all night to make a few more zlotis. And he

contributed a lot to the family's income. It was only later on, after the liberation, that he took seriously to painting. His was a pure talent that never received professional training. He produced many oil paintings: of clowns, fruits, still life.

He also painted biblical scenes. The most beautiful and the most important painting he created was a copy of *Isaac Blesses Jacob* by Govert Flink. The original is in the Rijksmuseum; Flink was a pupil of Rembrandt. Meyer worked hard on this picture after we had come to Montreal. It was a hot summer. He sat on our balcony on Trans Island Avenue, concentrating hard.

When I was recently in Amsterdam, I went into the Rijksmuseum. After I gazed at *The Nightwatchman* and other masterpieces, I came into a room and saw the very painting that my brother had copied. The original of *Isaac Blesses Jacob* is exactly the same size, with the same thick frame. I could have sworn that they took the painting from my living room and put it into the museum. It is completely identical. It is so magnificent that whoever comes to my house can't get over it. And Mayer painted it with no training whatsoever.

He was an artist in many other ways. He liked to paint beautiful women. He wasn't married, and only went out with beautiful women. He never went out with a girl who was not elegant. He was very sensitive, and this is the reason he never got married. He always only liked the beauty.

Motel

I also had another brother whose name was Motel. In Hebrew his name was Mordecai.

Motel worked hard as a controller for a business. Even though he worked for many hours, he was also very artistic and enjoyed drawing. Before the Jews of Lodz were sent to the Ghetto, he had married a gorgeous woman who came from an extremely poor family. Poor girls usually did not have much of a chance to marry without a dowry, but for our family, the dowry of a woman wasn't the most important thing.

My brother had told my parents, "Somehow I will try to make a living. But I must marry this girl." They soon had two children. Unfortunately, one child died later in the Ghetto from starvation; he didn't have enough milk.

### Isaac, the Oldest

I had yet an older brother, older than Motel. He too married a beautiful but poor girl. He loved her very much but unfortunately, three months after his wedding, he passed away of typhoid. There was no cure, no penicillin. His wife was already pregnant, and she gave birth to a son after his father's death. My brother's son was a beautiful boy, named sadly after his father.

What happened to him? He was called up during a "selection" in the Ghetto. They took him away from his mother, and we never heard from him again.

Now can one imagine what went on in the hearts of those women, those mothers, whose children were taken away by force? Some of them were so small, and they were thrown out on the track, thrown up by force.

It is now almost impossible, almost impossible to imagine what went on at that time, merely sixty years ago. And later the same thing happened to adults. They were taken from the streets and shipped them away to Auschwitz, or to Treblinka, or to other camps. They were simply going home from work, from their work for the Germans. Their suffering in the Ghetto was not enough for the Germans.

When the Germans wanted to liquidate the ghetto, they announced a *Spere*, a curfew. They wouldn't allow anyone to be in the streets. If the Nazis found someone outside, they went into a rage and raided the houses in the neighbourhood, shooting anyone who refused their new orders to go outside. They would round up the Jews and bring them to an Umschlagplatz, to a place from which they shipped them to the trains, to the freight trains that went to Auschwitz.

They were murderers. Their deeds were murderous, monstrous. For making innocent people suffer in such a terrible way, and for taking away their children: for this alone, I do not think that they deserve to have a nation today. I think that all of Germany should have become a parking lot. This is what they deserved, in my opinion.

And now, today, I have just two brothers left here in Montreal with me. One is Hyman, and the other is Sam. Hyman is a cantor and Sam is a businessman.

# *Memories of My Mother and Father*

My Mother, of Blessed Memory

My mother was a very, very beautiful woman, and so was her character. She suffered an awful lot from not having enough to give to her children. And I never heard her complain. Even though my father never succeeded in providing for his family, she never, never criticized him.

She always used to say, "The good things do not last forever, and the bad things do not last forever."

She married my father when she was eighteen years young, indeed a very young girl even for those days. Despite her youth, she came from a home where education played the highest role. She was fluent in Russian, Polish, and even in Hebrew, in writing and speaking.

My mother and my father were very religious people but not to the point of being fanatic. They did not ask us to wear earlocks like the other Hasidic youngsters.

No one in the family ever worked on Shabbat, no matter how drastic the economic hardship. I remember when one of my brothers lost a job, and our financial situation became very grim. My unmarried sister Eva was at the time offered a job in a store that sold umbrellas. Her job offer came just at a time when we really needed the extra income. But because she would not work on Shabbat—not one of us would dream of working on Shabbat—she declined the position. None of us would put my parents to the test.

But when this happened, I could not remain silent. With anger, I asked my mother, "Is it not a bigger sin for a family to suffer than for one of us to work on Shabbat?"

And then came the answer: "Didn't you learn *The Ethics of the Fathers?* There are no degrees when it comes to *mitzvoth*, or good deeds. There are also no degrees of *averot* (sins). Sometimes you think some act is just a small, little transgression. But in reality it could be that through this little misgiving, you come to do something much more serious." And then she continued: "I know that you are always complaining about the amount of hardships we have. There is never enough food, never enough clothing, no dowry for Eva. But let me explain something to you."

She looked at me intently. I heard every word she said: "This world of ours is like a corridor. You go through it in order to come to the main dining room. The psalmist says, 'Our days are no more than seventy years, and maybe even eighty.' When good and righteous people are suffering, the real reward will come in the next world, the hereafter. And the more we suffer here, the greater will be our reward." And then she told me the following story.

A rich man came from America to visit his father's grave in a small town in Poland. It happened to be the place where the great rabbi and scholar, the Chofetz Chaim, lived and taught. The rabbi greeted the American very warmly and offered him a glass of tea (in those days, they didn't drink tea out of a cup; truly, drinking it out of a glass tastes better!).

While the man was sipping the tea, he noticed how old and shabby the rabbi's furniture was. So he took courage and asked, "Rabbi, you are recognized all over the world as the greatest rabbi of your time. Why, then, is your furniture so old and shabby? Isn't it time to change this old furniture and live a little bit better?"

The rabbi replied by asking a question in turn: "How do *you* live in America? Do you have a nice house?"

The American said, "Sure, of course."

"You must have beautiful furniture too."

The American said, "Sure."

"So, why didn't you bring your furniture here?" the rabbi asked.

The man looked at the rabbi incredulously. "What kind of a question is this? I'm here only temporarily!"

And the rabbi quietly answered, "So am I."

But then, to make me feel a little better, my mother continued by saying this to me:

"My wonderful son, bad things are not forever, and good things are not forever. It's true that you are suffering right now, but there may come a time when things will become even much better." I begged her with childish impatience, "When?"

She said, "Soon."


A Memory of My Father

I must have been fifteen years old when my father could not take the embarrassment of not being able to make a living for his family. He decided to leave Lodz to try to find work somewhere else.

In those days, the mail didn't arrive regularly. Where we

lived, the mail was picked up just once a week.

The atmosphere at home was very subdued all throughout my father's absence. But soon we realized that my mother had not received any news from my father for weeks. And she simply felt devastated. And terribly worried.

Once in the middle of the night I heard my mother sobbing in the next room. When I came in, I saw my mother sitting up in bed, reciting *Tehillim*—psalms—quietly. She practically knew the psalms by heart. At the same time, she was crying bitterly.

Naturally I became very upset myself. And I tried to console my mother, begging her not to take it so hard and assuring her that any day the mail would arrive and that everything would be fine.

Unfortunately, days and weeks went by, and we still heard nothing from my father. It was not like today, when wherever you are, you can pick up the phone and get a call from as far away as China or Timbuktu. In those days, very few people— only the wealthy—had a phone.

And finally, one day a letter came. It was dated five weeks earlier. And the news was not too encouraging. My father told us later when he finally came home that he had tried very hard to get a position as a clergyman, a rabbi, but small towns did not have the funds to engage him.

At times on his journey, he could not find anyone who would even invite him in for a meal. And many times he went hungry, not even having a piece of bread to eat. But for my mother, it was enough that he came home safely.

# Hyman and Sam

My brothers Hyman and Sam survived by sheer luck. From the beginning of the war, they were convinced that it was their destiny to stay alive. Their faith in this idea gave them some of their strength to survive their ordeals, especially their horrific experiences in Dachau.

When the Lodz Ghetto was liquidated in 1944, Hyman and Sam were shipped off to Birkenau. From there, the Germans divided their prisoners among various camps. And so my brothers were sent to Dachau, to a branch of Dachau called Kaufering.

Dachau, of course, offered them the worst of circumstances, and they were expected to work under inhumane conditions. There was not enough food and not enough clothing. In the beginning, they still had a little bit of hope. "Maybe we will be free one day; maybe the war will end," they used to dream.

As it happened, however, the situation only became worse.

The seasons went on, and they didn't receive appropriate clothing. Worst of all for working, they were never given shoes. Sam, the younger one, went to work in the snow, and was expected to live without shoes when his one old pair fell apart. The sole was gone, so my other brother, who was very handy, found a piece of wood which he used to create a new sole. He tried to fasten it with wire so that the shoe would hold together at least while my brother stood at work in the snow.

Sam was afraid to take his shoes off at night, because in the morning he wouldn't have the time to fasten his homemade sole on correctly. When they would be woken up at four a.m., with the SS shouting, "*Schnell, schnell!* Hurry, hurry!" he was afraid he wouldn't have time to put on the wire, so he slept with those shoes on, with the wire digging into his feet. The result was that he soon he developed a terrible abscess, with pus, and he couldn't walk at all.

The camp doctor had nothing to work with—no anesthesia or medicine. He didn't even have bandages. Sam nearly gave up, crying out all the time in terrible pain. However, there was a Hungarian Jew in the barracks who knew a little bit about nursing, and this man said, "Your abscess has to be cut out. If you don't cut it off, you will get an infection all over your body and they will have to amputate your leg." The Hungarian man then took a knife, a simple knife from the kitchen. He sharpened it as well as he could. Two people had to hold my brother down so that he could not move. They held him tightly while the man cut out the entire abscess.

But then he couldn't find a bandage. However, the resourceful man looked about and decided to devise a bandage out of cement sacks. The cement sacks had three layers, and between the outer and inner layer is one additional layer that is cleaner than the others. So the men tore the sack open and made bandages from this middle part. Somehow Sam's wound began to heal.

But he wasn't cured for long. Soon after, he developed a similar abscess near his groin. This sore was even more difficult to remove. Sam went to work in pain, until he finally couldn't stand it any longer.

Sam and Hyman were thrown into a barracks where the sickest people were kept. The men he was with were deathly ill, each with a different sickness. But someone there told him that he too had once had an abscess. This man, like the Hungarian, took a knife and a similar bandage from a cement sack. Somehow this stopped the infection.

But often, too often, life did not seem worth living. Pestilence reined in the unit where my brothers were placed. There were lice crawling all over the bunks, so much lice that the blankets moved and vibrated even when no one was lying under them. Both Hyman and Sam soon became sick with typhoid fever.

The disease was so terrible that they began to lose their senses. They didn't have any water, anything to drink. They couldn't eat at all and their fevers rose to dangerously high temperature. They grew delirious. Most of the time they didn't know what they were saying to each other. All they remember are the high fevers, and the begging for a little water, for something moist to cool their fever.

With their dry thirst, they could not even bear to eat the tiny portions of bread that they received each day. But luckily for them, the bread was growing putrid, completely green with mould. They forced themselves to eat this dreadful meal when they received a little water. Because of this strange concoction, they survived their illnesses. They said that this green mould was like penicillin.

Finally, the Americans came close and the Nazis wanted to get rid of their Jewish prisoners. They took them out of the camp, throwing them all onto freight trains. Who knows where they were going? While my brothers were being shipped out, there was a sudden bomb alarm, and all the SS guards ran away fearfully in different directions.

This could have been a fortunate event, but for most of the prisoners it meant the end of their existence on earth. The train stopped in the middle of a field, only to confront an attack by the Allied forces. The pilots flying above the train thought that the trains held the retreating Nazi army. They dove down ferociously and shot the poor Jews aboard. When the attack was all over, my two brothers lifted up their heads cautiously.

With shock, they noticed that their whole train wagon, containing fifty or sixty people, had become a collection of dead bodies. Hyman and Sam had lifted their heads only to realize that they were the only ones who had survived this ordeal. They were the only ones not shot.

They were very weak. Tall men, they now weighed only about twenty-five kilos each. They threw themselves back down on the ground, and lay there until a truck arrived with a group of SS guards. The SS picked up my brothers and transported them to yet another camp, from which they were eventually liberated.

They spent many months recuperating in the hospital. It was there that they found out about us. It was through a sheer miracle and tremendous coincidence that they found out that we were alive. If it hadn't been for the man who recognized the connection, they could have moved to somewhere else. We might never have heard from them even to this very day. We might never have known that we had two brothers still alive.

# *Aftermath*

Even today I still don't know what happened to the children of my other brothers. Maybe some of them are still alive. We never could find out because they were so young when the war occurred. Perhaps I have nieces and nephews who did not know that we had a cousin in Israel. We all remembered throughout the horrible years that we had a cousin who had settled in Israel. After the war, we contacted him many times. If only these relatives knew, they could have contacted us. But apparently, either they didn't remember or they are not here. It is a very miserable feeling always to think that someone close to you might not know that you exist.

My wife Anna tried as well to locate her family to see if someone had survived. Unfortunately, she always came back with the same answer: they can't find anyone. And this was a very frustrating thing, to know that even though you are married, you have no family that you can count on. No uncles, no cousins, no distant cousins. *Someone* must exist! But she was very young when her parents gave her away to the Gentile family.

Anna depended on me to be her family. She always said that if she hadn't met and married me, she wouldn't have survived. She would simply have taken her life, so frustrating it was. And lonesome.

And yet how horrid the irony is. When Anna applied to get some restitution from the German government in 1956, she was denied because she couldn't remember the name of the first camp where she had been sent. She had been very confused, very alone, and very young. The Germans first granted her some restitution, then stopped, and wouldn't give her a pension.

This was after she had lost her parents, her whole family. Naturally, her fate in the camps deprived her of any education. But what good is restitution after all? Is a few hundred dollars a month repayment for having worked as a slave for four-and-a-half years? As slave workers for the SS, we were treated even worse than slaves. We didn't get enough food, didn't get enough clothing.

For a few hundred dollars they think that they can buy back our innocence. They think that we are all right now.

As a matter of fact, I have a friend who never wanted to receive a penny from the German government. He said, "They can never pay me off for the loss of my whole family's lives, and for the suffering that I went through for five years. I won't let them buy my innocence and cure their guilt feelings with money."

He was quite right. But some of us unfortunately needed the money and couldn't resist taking it. But each time we receive it, it is with a bitter taste in our mouth.

The Germans who want to pay us now are the same who ruined and broke my friends. I had a friend in camp who was a very, very jovial person. He was always optimistic, no matter how hard the times were. He received the same treatment we went through, but never seemed to complain. He was always hungry but he always tried to think about the future, as he was convinced that life was going to be better one day. He had a great sense of humor. At times when we were not feeling like laughing, he managed to make us laugh. A wonderful fellow. This man survived the war, and I met him later on.

"How are you doing?" I asked him, expecting to hear great news.

He said, however, "Not so good. They castrated me." They did this for experimental purposes. I wonder: how much money do they owe a person like this, whose life they ruined forever?

Gone was his humor, gone was his hope. He had nothing to live for. I no longer know where he is; he left for Australia perhaps. I lost contact but I still wonder: how much money do they have to pay him in order to pay for their guilt?

I had another close friend with whom I was in the Baylitz camp. I actually owe my life to him. He was working in the kitchen, and he told my brother and me that whenever we came for our dinner soup, we should line up in a single line to be counted. The guard would count the number of people in the line, and then he would count the number of bowls that people were carrying. He said, "Come with two bowls, not just one. And tell your brother to do the same thing." Why? "Because one bowl will be under your windbreaker. Get yourself a windbreaker. You'll say someone is sick in the barracks and couldn't get to the kitchen." Our method worked for quite a time, probably for a few months, or up to a year.

This man, Morris Goldlust, became a successful businessman in Toronto. Today he has a wife, wonderful children and grandchildren. And whenever we meet, I remind him that I owe my life to him. His help for us was like winning the lotto. Having a little extra soup in those days could mean the difference between life and death.

# *Final Reflections*

It is usual that you make the small decisions, but the big decisions somehow are made for you and are out of your control. These decisions seem to come from God. Everything works out in a different way than you had expected.

# *About the Author*

When Solomon Gisser and his pregnant wife Anna arrived in Canada in 1952, they were penniless. After living for a time on $15 a week from the Jewish Immigrant Aid Services, he was hired as cantor for the Shaare Zion Synagogue in Montreal, where he served for forty-five years. An accomplished singer of opera and Yiddish songs, Cantor Gisser has been in constant demand outside the synagogue as well. He has performed with the Montreal Symphony Orchestra and has sung five times at the Montreal Forum to audiences of 20,000 people. He has given recitals in Israel and is the recipient of an Honorary Fellowship from the Jewish Theological Seminary. His son David is an attorney in Winnipeg, and his daughter Helen lives in Boca Raton, Florida. Cantor Gisser has three grandchildren.

# *About the Editor*

David Patterson holds the Bornblum Chair of Excellence in Judaic Studies at The University of Memphis and is Director of Bornblum Judaic Studies. He is the author of *Along the Edge of Annihilation, Sun Turned to Darkness, The Greatest Jewish Stories Ever Told, When Learned Men Murder, Pilgrimage of a Proselyte: From Auschwitz to Jerusalem, The Shriek of Silence* and other books. He is also co-editor of the *Encyclopedia of Holocaust Literature* and is a Winner of the Koret Jewish Book Award.